CONFESSIONS *of a* BOOK REVIEWER

ALA Editions purchases fund advocacy, awareness, and accreditation programs for library professionals worldwide.

Confessions *of a* BOOK REVIEWER

The Best of Carte Blanche

MICHAEL CART

Foreword by Francesca Lia Block

A BOOKLIST PUBLICATION

ALA Editions
An imprint of the
AMERICAN LIBRARY ASSOCIATION
Chicago • 2018

Michael Cart is a columnist and reviewer for *Booklist* magazine and the author or editor of twenty-four books. He is a past president of both the Young Adult Library Services Association and ALAN (Assembly on Literature for Adolescents of the National Council of Teachers of English). Cart has taught young adult literature at UCLA and lectures nationally on the subject. He is the recipient of the Grolier Award and the YALSA/Greenwood Publishing Group Services to Young Adults' Achievement Award. He earned a bachelor's degree from Northwestern University and a master's degree from Columbia University.

ISBNs
978-0-8389-1645-2 (paper)
978-0-8389-1674-2 (PDF)
978-0-8389-1673-5 (ePub)
978-0-8389-1675-9 (Kindle)

Library of Congress Cataloging in Publication Control Number: 2017050589

Cover design by Kimberly Thornton; imagery © Adobe Stock. Text design and composition by Karen Sheets de Gracia in the Meta Serif and Corki typefaces.

∞ This paper meets the requirements of ANSI/NISO Z39.48–1992 (Permanence of Paper).

Printed in the United States of America

22 21 20 19 18 5 4 3 2 1

CONTENTS

INTRODUCTION

ONE DAY IN the spring of 1994 my telephone rang. To my surprise it was Bill Ott, editor and publisher of *Booklist* magazine, calling. I had met Bill but didn't know him well, so I presumed he wasn't calling just to chat or talk about those Cubs. My presumption was correct: to my amazement he was calling to invite me—out of the blue—to do a monthly column for *Booklist*. I considered his invitation for approximately five seconds before I said "Yes." I might have added "Try and stop me," because to do a column was a lifelong dream of mine. It began when I was a boy, a boy who—I'm fond of saying—would read anything that didn't get up and walk away. My reading ranged from cereal boxes to the daily newspaper, from classics to comics. Somewhere in the middle was my mother's monthly copy of the magazine *Better Homes and Gardens*. Mind you, I wasn't that interested in homes and gardens, either better or worse; no, what interested me was a feature that appeared on the final page of each issue: a column called "The Man Next Door" written by Burton Hillis (years later I discovered this was a pseudonym for William E. Vaughan, who also wrote for *The Reader's Digest*). The column was a cheerfully anecdotal report of his family's small adventures in suburbia, accompanied by some homespun aphorisms; for example, "Suburbia is where the developer bulldozes out the trees, then names the streets after them"; "A real patriot is the fellow who gets a parking ticket and rejoices that the system works." And—well, you get the idea. I enjoyed it so much that I found myself thinking how great it would be to write a column of my own someday. Flash forward forty or so years and I found that my dream had just come true!

Twenty-three years have passed since Bill's phone call and its genesis of the column that has come to be called Carte Blanche. During that time I've written more than 250 columns about a great gallimaufry of topics (it's not for nothing that the column is called Carte Blanche), though all have, in their respective ways, dealt thematically with sundry aspects of books, reading, writing, and publishing, a fact that lends some unity and coherence to what would otherwise be a ragtag assemblage.

Inevitably, some things about the column have changed over the years. In the early days I was, at most, a shadowy presence in them; I always took a back seat to whatever topic I was addressing, yet somehow I gradually started to move out of the shadows and onto the page, especially when I was discussing books, and that gave rise to a series of columns in which I wrote about my own collections and more often than not—since I'm a peripatetic person—about the act of moving when you own upwards of 15,000 books. You'll find a gathering of such columns in the chapter I'm calling—what else?—"Books, Books, Books." Aside from an infusion of me, me, me, what else has changed in the columns? Well, one thing has been my growing passion for young adult literature. In the early years it wasn't uncommon for me to devote a column or three to some aspect of children's literature, which was—after all—my first passion as a reader. But gradually young adult literature has moved center stage, in part because of my love for it but also, more pragmatically, because that field has become so, yes, vast that it's almost impossible to keep abreast of its every aspect, let alone that of children's literature. You won't find evidence of it in this book—except in its title—but in addition to being a columnist, I'm also a reviewer for *Booklist,* specializing in young adult literature and, increasingly, in adult books as well, though this last is a topic for another time. The bottom line is that I'm consumed with young adult literature and my columns reflect that. One thing hasn't changed, however, and that's my seeming obsession with my age! I was a mere stripling of 53 when I began the column; over the years people have watched me age until, now, I have reached a spirited 76. No matter my age, however, I'd like to think that over the years I have revealed a sense of humor and I hope, accordingly, that I've been able to invest most of my columns with some salutary wit (this is where some wise guy says, "Well, at least he's half right, har har har"). As for style, thanks to a degree in journalism (I graduated from Northwestern University's Medill School of Journalism), I've tried to affect an accessible, easygoing expository style, sprinkled with some polysyllables when they have seemed irresistibly apposite (see what I mean?).

Given the parameters I've outlined above, I really have had carte blanche to write about whatever has excited my interest, though if you're a regular reader of my home base, *Booklist,* you'll know that each of its issues focuses on a spotlight topic such as Historical Fiction, Graphic Novels, Mystery, and so on. Most of the time my columns will spotlight the same subject; that is, if the issue's focus is on Mystery, my column will explore some aspect of Mystery. The words "some aspect" are central here, because they give me lots of latitude in my approach. That's the good news. The bad news is that after you've written half-a-dozen columns about—say—Romance, you tend to repeat yourself if you're not careful—especially if, like me, you have about as much romance in your soul as a turnip, and a short memory. That said, my columns doubtless reveal a sentimental streak as wide as the state of Texas. I'm fond of saying that—like former President Clinton—I'll cry at the grand opening of a car wash! Anyway, though it sometimes takes a bit of heavy lifting, I think I've managed to keep my approaches original. You'll be the judge of that when you read the columns this book contains.

About those columns: you'll find fifty of them here. I'd like to think they comprise the best of the best of the more than 250 I've visited on you over the years. For ease of access I've organized them into the eight different categories you'll discover when you take a gander at the Table of Contents. Of course, my columns have explored far more than eight categories over the years, so obviously some didn't make the cut; oftentimes those are ones that seem dated because of their focus on individual titles or topics of the moment. Thus, for example, you won't find any of my Columnist's Choice columns in which I've offered my selections of the best books of the year; nor will you find any of the columns I've written about annual American Library Association (ALA) conferences. No, forget the timely; instead I've striven for the—dare I say it?—timeless.

Have I succeeded? You tell me. Welcome to Carte Blanche.

FOREWORD

I MET MICHAEL CART soon after my first book *Weetzie Bat* was published by Charlotte Zolotow at Harper Collins (then Harper & Row). I was in my twenties, recently graduated from UC Berkeley, and new to the world of publishing. I didn't even know that I was writing a "young adult" book and had intended Weetzie for an older, smaller audience of artists, punk rockers and Los Angelinos, rather than for teens. As I tried to navigate this new world, Michael came to my rescue. He was the elegant, urbane mentor I needed. My beloved artist father, who had always championed my work, had just died and I cast Michael in the role of an avuncular guide. But I also saw Michael as a colleague, a friend, and, dare I admit, a bit of a crush. He was so handsome, charming, and kind! Michael had written the quintessential review that launched my book. He drove me to one library event and, on the way, he talked to me about his mystical experiences with meditation and offered his astute theories on the possible psychology behind my book *The Hanged Man*. Later he interviewed me for his cable author interview show, *In Print*. Though I was sick with anxiety about being on camera, he made me feel at ease. He also wrote a biography about me as part of a series on the lives of various writers, featured my *Weetzie Bat* in one of his Carte Blanche columns, and asked me to contribute stories to two anthologies he edited. Later, when I began to focus on my adult work, he supported that as well. I believe he had more than a little to do with my receiving the Margaret A. Edwards Lifetime Achievement Award in 2005, an honor that changed my career and my life.

Michael Cart is a wonderful author, editor, critic, journalist, columnist, historian, librarian, and television star. (And I do mean star.) Most of all, he has been a mentor and friend at the times I needed one most.

Francesca Lia Block

Los Angeles, 2017

PREFACE

In the Beginning: The Column That Started It All

I WAS QUICK to accept Bill Ott's invitation to become a *Booklist* columnist without thinking much about consequences. Those were among the things I faced when I sat down to write my first column. What on earth would I write about, and how would I go about actually doing it? It was, after all, my first time out of the gate and I wanted to hit the ground running. Despite my metaphors, I quickly dismissed the idea of writing about race horses, but what else would serve? Serendipity provided the answer, for there at my elbow was a copy of American poet Donald Hall's *Life Work,* a then newly published memoir-cum-meditation about the life of the writer and a love for the past that I shared. It inspired me to seek out other examples of his work, notably such children's books as *Ox-Cart Man, The Man Who Lived Alone,* and *The Farm Summer 1942.* Eureka! I would write about Donald Hall. And, readers, so I did. Here's the result, "The Great Cavern of Old Time," my maiden voyage as a writer. Hmmm, perhaps I should write my next column about ships . . .

The Great Cavern of Old Time

I planned long ago I would live here, somebody's grandfather.

—*Donald Hall*

THESE WORDS, WHICH I serendipitously discovered while browsing the pages of poet Donald Hall's 1978 book *Kicking the Leaves* (Harper), brought me up short because they say so much about the man I had just gotten to know through the pages of his more recent book, *Life Work* (Beacon, 1993). This engrossing memoir-cum-meditation about the work of writing and the enormous place it occupies in the poet's personal life goes a long way toward explaining why a critic has called Hall "one of the most thorough literary professionals in America."

Anyone who has read *Life Work* will readily understand that the two most important words in that line quoted above are "here" and "grandfather." "Here" is the old farmhouse on Eagle Pond in the shadow of New Hampshire's Ragged Mountain, where Hall and his wife, the poet Jane Kenyon, make their home, while "grandfather" invokes the spirit of Hall's own beloved grandparent, a man with the nicely alliterative name of Wesley Wells, who lived—with his wife, Kate—in that same house when Hall was a boy.

"He was my model," Hall writes, and one supposes he was the shaper of the poet's ear as well, since Wesley was in the habit of telling stories and reciting poetry out loud while he worked at farming as a then-young Donald helped him through a "decade of summers, 1940 to 1950."

The experiences of that decade have now been delightfully encapsulated in Hall's newest children's book, *The Farm Summer 1942*. The book tells the simple but affecting story of the summer that a nine-year-old San Francisco boy named Peter spends on a New Hampshire farm with his grandparents while his father and mother are busy with the war effort. Peter helps with the haying, feeds the chickens, listens to his grandfather tell stories and recite poems, reads his father's boyhood books, and finally—at summer's end—returns home to the city by the bay with the promise of another farm visit the following year.

The art in this quiet book resides in the ginger snaps and rhubarb pie, in the milk toast and the Moxie, in the buggy and the gull rake, in all the closely observed details of daily living that capture, entire, the experience and the era.

That experience is enriched by Barry Moser's sympathetic watercolor illustrations. If some of these have the flat, posed quality of snapshots from an aging family album, that is only appropriate to a story that is itself composed of scenes which have been preserved in the amber of the author's memory.

A similar kind of art informs my own favorite among Hall's growing body of books for children: *The Man Who Lived Alone* (Godine, 1984). This hauntingly understated tale of a solitary man who lives in his camp on Ragged Mountain was inspired—as we learn in *Life Work*—by the real life of Freeman Morrison, a cousin of Hall's grandmother who embodied in his first name and in his habits the persistent American dream of self-sufficiency. His ruggedly independent days are beautifully evoked in Hall's poetic, almost elegiac prose and Mary Azarian's woodcut illustrations.

Hall has been persistently lucky in the illustrators with whom he has worked; indeed, one of them—Barbara Cooney—won the Caldecott Medal for her contributions to his most famous children's book, *Ox-Cart Man* (Viking, 1979).

Meanwhile, Michael McCurdy has executed amazingly apposite, color scratchboard pictures for the hardworking Hall's next two books: *Lucy's Christmas* and *Lucy's Summer.* For their inspiration, the author turned to the long-ago girlhood of his now ninety-year-old mother. The "Lucy" books will be published in fall 1994 and spring 1995 by Browndeer Press, Linda Zuckerman's imprint at Harcourt.

Zuckerman shares my enthusiasm for Donald Hall's work. In fact, this normally serious and reserved professional becomes positively ebullient when she talks about the joys of working with a remarkable writer who is "very clear about who he is and what he wants to do but is, nevertheless, very open to other points of view and who relishes the idea of revisions and of polishing a manuscript."

She will publish a third brightly polished book by Hall in the fall of 1995. To be illustrated by Barry Moser, this book's title, *The Legend of Babe Ruth,* betrays the poet's steadfast devotion to our national pastime. In fact, Zuckerman tells me, Hall will be one of the featured commentators in the forthcoming PBS series about baseball that is being produced by Ken Burns, who gave us last season's memorable series about the Civil War.

It's suitable to share, in closing, one last thing Hall has to say about his late grandfather. He thanks him for being, as he puts it, "my source or entrance into the great cavern of old-time."

Hats off to Donald Hall himself for so generously sharing the treasures he has found in that cavern in the pages of his wonderfully artful books for children.

I don't know what Hall's grandparents looked like, but I wouldn't be surprised if they resembled the people who appear in photographer Archie Lieberman's new book, *Neighbors* (Collins San Francisco, 1993). Lieberman first visited Scales Mound, Illinois, in 1954 on assignment for *This Week* magazine. He was so captivated by the Hammers, one of the farm families he met there, that he decided to make a photographic record of their lives. The result was *Farm Boy,* which was published by Abrams in 1974. Now he continues that record and adds to it pictures of the Hammers' neighbors. These moving black-and-white images haunt the memory and demonstrate the powerful beauty of faces that are no strangers to punishingly hard work and weather. Though published as an adult book, *Neighbors* is a perfect companion to Donald Hall's stories about rural America.

Similarly, the love Hall demonstrates for the landscape and the multi-generational families who work it is wonderfully complemented by Newbery medalist Patty MacLachlan's newest book, *All the Places to Love*, illustrated by Mike Wimmer and published by HarperCollins. It is a sweet-spirited evocation by a boy named Eli of his earliest memories of the family farm, of its meadows and hay fields, its hilltop "where the blackberries grew," its river "where the woods began"—in short, of all the places there to love.

I predict that readers will love them, too.

June 1 and 15, 1994 • *Booklist*

1

ON READING AND WRITING

Passions and Pleasures

SOMEONE ONCE CALLED me "phlegmatic"; it wasn't meant as a compliment. But it wasn't altogether accurate, either. I have my passions, thank you very much, reading chief among them. I've been an avid reader for—count 'em—sixty-nine years and, God willing, I'm prepared to be for another sixty-nine years. Why am I so passionate about reading? Let poet and critic T. S. Eliot provide an answer: In his *Notes Towards the Definition of Culture* he wrote that there are three "permanent" reasons for reading: 1, the acquisition of wisdom; 2, the enjoyment of art; and 3, the pleasure of entertainment. Now, I don't know that I have done so well with the first reason (the person who once said, "We grow too soon old and too late smart" was looking at me!), but I've gone to town on reasons 2 and 3. You want pleasures? I've got pleasures. They're called "books." So consider the columns in this chapter my love songs to reading, a difficult and complex art but one close to my heart.

The Paradigms, They Are A-Shiftin'

"FOR EVERY READER who dies today, a viewer is born," Jonathan Franzen points out in a recent *New Yorker* review of *The Gutenberg Elegies,* Sven Birkerts's thought-provoking collection of essays about the state of reading in America. Franzen is referring to Birkerts's premise that we late-twentieth-century types are living in the midst of a paradigm shift—a wrenching movement from a print-based culture to one based, instead, on virtual images. This seismic shift began with television and is being completed by computers. Thus, "in print" is being replaced by "online," and the trouble with that, for us resolute readers, is that the new technology demands too little of our imaginations, turning us into passive observers instead of the active collaborators we used to be. Or, as Birkerts puts it, "When you read a novel, much of the color, sound and motion come from you, the reader."

Ironically, this shift comes at the very time when the teaching of reading has become the subject of much debate, fired by the fact that fewer and fewer young people demonstrate any talent for the increasingly arcane art. Reading is becoming alchemy; we dimly remember that this mysterious process can produce gold, but we've forgotten that we have the philosopher's stone already at hand: it's called a book.

I certainly don't pretend to be an expert on the teaching of reading, but as a Californian, I was intrigued several years ago by the reports from our state capital of the advent of a literature based method of instruction called "whole language." That capital, you may recall, is Sacramento, where gold was discovered in the middle of the last century. Now, in the wake of the latter-day rush to whole language, there are those who are grumpily declaring that all that glitters is not gold, and the movement, to mix a nice metaphor, has turned into a political football to be tossed back and forth between its champions and those who yearn for a return to the good old days of phonics, rote instruction, and the basal days and doings of Dick and Jane. To politicize an issue is to run the two-pronged risk of oversimplifying and overlaying it with so many passions and agendas that rational and dispassionate discussion becomes impossible.

That's a pity, because we need to talk about reading and about why so many young people today, unable or unwilling to do it, are shortchanging themselves. For if literacy is currency in our society, too many folks are impoverished, and if you doubt it, look at the results of a 1993 U.S. Department of Education study titled *Adult Literacy in America*. This first-ever national literacy survey revealed that 49 percent of adult Americans can now be described as functionally illiterate and that 41 to 44 percent of those who tested in the lowest skill levels live in poverty. The future looks equally bleak: the survey confirmed that the literacy skills of young adults are also in decline; those who participated in the 1993 survey tested 11 to 14 points lower than young adults tested in 1985. It is now estimated that a quarter of America's high-school seniors can barely read their diplomas, while 80 percent of the juvenile offenders who appear in U.S. courts are functionally illiterate. It would be wrongheaded to lay all the blame for these statistics on the emergence of electronic culture, but I think it is significant that when Birkerts taught an undergraduate course in 1992, he was discouraged to discover that most of his students were not readers. "They had always occupied themselves with music, TV, and videos," he notes, and accordingly "they had difficulty slowing down enough to concentrate on prose of any density."

At the same time I was reading this disturbing assessment, I was reading a book by another teacher: the Frenchman Daniel Pennac, whose book *Better Than Life* was the number-one bestseller in France in 1993. Encountering a similar resistance to reading among his students, Pennac muses, "it looks as though school, no matter the age or nation, has had only one role. And that's to teach the mastery of technique and critical commentary and to cut off spontaneous contact with books by discouraging the pleasure of reading. You learn how to read at school," he concludes, "but what about the love of reading?" His answer was to encourage reading aloud in his classroom. "A teacher who reads out loud lifts you to the level of books. He gives you the gift of reading."

This passage reminded me of an essay called "Bring Back the Out-Loud Culture" by the poet Donald Hall. It begins, "As a boy in the 1940s, I stood in the tie-up watching my New Hampshire grandfather milk holsteins while he recited poems for my entertainment. His hands stripped milk to the poem's beat. He threw back his head, rolled his eyes in high drama and pounded out: 'But there is no joy in Mudville—mighty Casey has struck out.'" Hall continues, "Before the late 1920s and 1930s American culture was out loud. We continually turned print into sound . . . but when we stopped memorizing and reciting literature, our ability to read started its famous decline. In order to become a nation of readers, we need again to become a nation of reciters."

I'm not sure how I learned to read nearly fifty years ago, but I remember that my mother habitually read to me and my twin sister before we started school. No wonder I grew up thinking there was something magical about hearing the sounds of language. The magic continued when I went to school. Some of my most vivid classroom memories are of being read to by my fourth- and fifth-grade teacher, Miss Beatty, and of subsequently sharing the read-aloud role with my sixth-grade teacher, Mr. Kimmel. Not that any of the books we shared in those Indiana classrooms were any great shakes as literature. I remember that Miss Beatty's favorite read-aloud title was an even-then antique novel called *The Song of the Cardinal* by Hoosier author Gene Stratton Porter, while Mr. Kimmel and I must have taken turns reading half-a-dozen Tarzan books to my sixth grade classmates. The literary quality of these texts was less important than what we listeners were intuitively learning: that, as Pennac puts it, the first job of the novel is to "quench our thirst for stories." Maybe that's the reason that for so many people, the best-loved books of their childhoods are ones that are inconsequential as literature but, in an intensely personal way, slaked that story thirst. Such satisfaction seems to be increasingly elusive as we hear, not the soul-stirring sounds of language, but the stultifying static of technobabble.

"How strange," Pennac observes, "that reading out loud has disappeared from our world." And how wonderful it would be to bring it and the joyful pleasure of reading books back to life.

January 1 and 15, 1996 • *Booklist*

Is Reading Selfish?

EACH YEAR IN this issue, *Booklist* publishes the ALA "best" and "notable" lists, including the Notable Books list for adults, the Notable Children's Book list, YALSA's Best Books and Quick Picks lists, and various media lists. And each year I have some fun second-guessing the choices of the hard-working committees that have assembled these lists. But this year I thought I'd do something a little different with my monthly space. The catalyst for such a radical departure from Carte Blanche tradition is a discussion strand that's currently filling my YALSA-BK in-basket brim-full with messages. The discussion began with a post from a librarian who—in the wake of non-stop perusal to prepare for a mock Printz discussion—posed a provocative question: Is reading, she asked, a selfish thing to do, in the sense that it is a solitary act that precludes the participant's doing other "valuable" things? And, if it is selfish, how can other librarians feel "good" about encouraging young people to do it? (This may be the only time the phrase "do it" has referred to reading, by the way.)

The fact that this posting stirred some sixty passionate responses in less than a week did my old heart good since it suggests that, even in an online age in which technology reigns as king, people still care about and are interested in the act of reading books. I received further evidence of this fact last week when, after giving a day-long presentation on young adult literature to an audience of Chicago-area librarians, one of them—a media specialist—thanked me warmly for giving her a day free of technology.

Hey, it was my pleasure.

Nevertheless, I was not one of the five dozen YALSA-BK respondents. I did read all the messages with keen interest, though, since I spend so much of my waking life reading—and writing. And both of these are solitary and, thus, perhaps, selfish acts. In fact, my late friend the poet and critic Myra Cohn Livingston used to worry aloud that she spent so much of her time reading and writing that she was in danger of becoming a hermit and, moreover, that she was short-changing her family in the process. Interestingly, the few respondents who allowed as how, yes, they might be selfish in their avid reading echoed this very reason.

Though I don't have an immediate family, I can understand this reservation. After all, I seize every available opportunity to fly to Indiana to spend some quality time with my three great-nephews, who are now seven, four, and three, respectively. Their idea of quality time is not reading, alas, but is, rather, running around the house, screaming. And since I don't get to see them very often, there I am too, running around after them and doing some merry screaming myself (and so much for people thinking I'm always "so dignified").

Speaking of sharing, I also share another problem expressed by many of the respondents, and by the kids with whom they work, for that matter: it seems harder and harder to find the time to read and write. Whenever I used to complain to Myra about that, she would give me one of "those" looks (if you knew her, you know the look I mean) and say, "Dear, you *find* the time to do the things you really want to do."

Okay, Myra. I really do want to read and write. And so my present strategy for finding the time is to get up at 4:00 in the morning seven days a week and read until about 7:30, when I repair to my home office, turn on the computer, and start writing. I also have a book with me whenever I leave the house so that I can read while stuck in traffic, while waiting in line at the supermarket (where having a book keeps me from reading those oh-so-tempting tabloids at the checkout stand), or while sitting on an airplane (speaking of things I really *don't* want to do). And yes, whenever I travel I now lug along my laptop so that I can write, too, during every period of downtime.

I do this because, the older I get, the more important I feel words are. Does this mean I'm becoming more selfish in my dotage? Nah. For, after all, my *American Heritage Dictionary* defines selfish as "concerned chiefly or only with oneself."

And to me, the chief importance, the greatest value of reading is that it takes you out of yourself and into the hearts, minds, and lives of other human beings. It expands your viewpoint, it broadens your horizons, it heightens your understanding of others, and in these ways it humanizes you.

The British literary critic Brian Alderson put it slightly differently some years ago when I asked him why he felt books and reading were important. Without hesitation, he responded, "Well, I suppose books are only important if you think reading is important; and I suppose reading is only important if you think civilization is important."

Amen, brother, amen.

How can you feel "good" about encouraging young people to engage in this solitary act? How can you feel "good" not encouraging them to read? Civilization depends on it.

That's why so many of the words I write are about books—and reading. I want to share my enthusiasm for both. And that's why I think lists of notable and best books are important, too. Time is too limited to waste on bad books (yes, there are lots of those!), but no single individual (not even me) has the time to examine and evaluate every new title that comes down the pike. So we must share our resources, we must parcel out our expertise; we must read, write, and react! For another of the glories of reading is the desire the act inspires to discuss what is being read and to interact with and relate to other human beings.

So is reading selfish? Heck, no. In fact, it's the most generous-spirited act I can imagine.

And thank goodness it is. Because civilization depends on it!

March 15, 2004 • *Booklist*

My Romance . . . with Reading

SO I'M IN the weight room at my gym yesterday, busily courting a double hernia, when my 25-year-old trainer—the young pup—says, "Are you ever going to retire?"

Well, there are a number of answers I could have given to that—most of them as rudely impertinent as the question—but I like to keep the discourse civil, and besides, the kid is bigger (and lots stronger) than I am. So I answered his question with one of my own: "Why should I retire?"

And then, before he could provide the obvious answer ("Because you're *old!*"), I smoothly answered myself: "After all, I love my work," I said.

And so I do.

Of course, I'm sometimes hard-pressed to explain exactly what that work is. I write, of course—this column, reviews, articles, essays, book-length works of literary criticism, the occasional short story, the even-more-occasional novel. I edit (my young adult literary journal *Rush Hour* and the occasional anthology). I teach (currently at UCLA, formerly at Texas Woman's University, prospectively at San Diego State University). I lecture all over the map (mostly on young adult literature, though occasionally I talk about young adults themselves). I consult (on publishing and libraries). I do a ton of pro bono and volunteer work (mostly for associations that serve librarians and educators). I . . . well, whatever it is that I do, it seems to keep me busy seven days a week. (I'm writing this on a Saturday morning, for example, while you're all still lounging around in designer robes and pajamas.) Of course, this means I don't have much time left over for a life, but that's okay because (pause) . . . because . . .

Wake up, people: this is the call-and-response part of the column: this is where you chorus, "*Because I love my work!*"

Geez. Talk about heavy lifting.

When I take a moment to contemplate the smorgasbord that is my professional résumé, however, I recognize that my tasks—no matter how seemingly disparate—have one thing in common: they all involve words, ideas, and communication.

That's the big picture. More specifically, though, my work consists of coming up with ideas, translating them into words—into a message, if you will—and then finding ways of communicating that message. (I knew that undergraduate degree in journalism would come in handy someday.)

Marshall McLuhan once famously said, "The medium is the message," but in my line o' work, the *message* is the message, and I will cheerfully use any medium available to convey it, even a megaphone through which I can shout on a street corner.

So I guess I could describe myself as a professional communicator. But I'm more than that. After all, where do my ideas come from? How did I learn to form them into words?

By reading, of course.

Let me say that again: by reading. And not just books.

I've had a lifelong *romance* with reading—with reading anything: books, magazines, newspapers, pamphlets, fliers, cereal boxes. *I love to read. I believe in reading.*

And this is where ideas, words, and communication come together in one fundamental message: Reading is simply the most important thing in the world.

Now we're getting down to the important stuff. Why do I think reading is so blamed important? Because reading is what civilizes us, that's why.

Someone once said, "We read to know we are not alone."

Yes. I agree. But to me that means we read to travel outside ourselves. (Note to editor: see how cleverly I managed to work both spotlight topics, romance and travel, into my column? NOW do I get a raise?) We read to know we are not alone because reading can transport us into other minds, into other lives, into other circumstances. We read to gain insight, to spark ideas, to engage in unspoken dialogue with the minds of authors and the characters they create.

So we read to gain information, knowledge, and—if we read long and thoughtfully enough—wisdom. So we read to educate the mind.

But we also read to educate the heart.

By which I mean we read to learn empathy, compassion, tolerance, understanding.

We read to learn that the sun does not rise and set solely on our own blessed selves. We read to learn that we are not the center of the universe.

And that, of course, is why it's so important for those citizens called "adolescents," "teenagers," and "young adults" to read. Because they are the quintessential solipsists; they, more than anybody else, need to be transported outside of themselves.

Unfortunately, because I believe so passionately in the importance of reading for everyone, but especially for young adults, the world keeps breaking my heart.

The latest heartbreak arrived recently in the form of a report from the National Endowment for the Arts, a report the NEA itself called "a bleak assessment" of the state of reading in the United States. You can read the sixty-page report for yourselves (it's available online at www.nea.gov/pub/ReadingAtRisk.pdf), but essentially, it concludes that the reading of literature in America is in precipitous decline and that the rate of decline is most precipitous among—you guessed it—18- to 24-year-olds.

Oh, joy.

The worst of it is that the report also finds that the less people read, the less they volunteer, the less they go to cultural events, the less they become engaged with information and society. In other words, the less civilized they become.

This is not good news, people. Its one upside is that my message just became more relevant. Reading is the most important thing in the world. Tell a friend. Tell a teenager! But don't just tell them. Show them by modeling reading behavior. Read publicly with evident appreciation, enjoyment, and gusto. If you're a parent, fill your house with books, magazines, and newspapers, and read them with your kids. If you're a teacher, read to your kids, and make time for silent sustained reading. If you're a librarian, hand-sell favorite books, talk to and with kids about books, start a book discussion group.

Do whatever it takes. But get them reading!

As for me? I'm already converted, and I promise you that I will never stop reading. Nor will I ever stop communicating my message about the importance of reading. It's more than my profession. It's my calling. In fact, when I finally shuffle off this mortal coil, you will have to pry a book out of my cold, dead hands. And so the real answer to my trainer's question—"Will you ever retire?"—is a resounding "Never!"

Never, never, never.

And when it comes to reading, I hope you won't either.

September 15, 2004 • *Booklist*

A Difficult and Complex Art

BOOKLIST'S ANNUAL LISTING of the year's notable books has started me thinking about the act of reading. Accordingly, I was intrigued by an article in the January 5, 2014, issue of the *New York Times*. Written by Colin Robinson, co-publisher of OR Books, it's headlined "The Loneliness of the Long-Distance Reader," and it offers some fascinating insights into the current condition of reading, books, and publishing. Not surprisingly, Robinson takes a gander at the impact of the Internet on all of this. He begins, though, with a pre-Internet 1925 quote from Virginia Woolf: "To read a novel is a difficult and complex art." He then goes on to say this: "Today, with our powers of concentration atrophied by the staccato communication of the Internet and attention easily diverted to addictive entertainment on our phones and tablets, book-length reading is harder still."

Now, I'm not an Internet addict, but I use the darned thing and, yes, I do find book-length reading harder than it used to be—bad news for a reviewer—and I do blame the Internet for compromising my concentration and shrinking my attention span. More and more these days, I find myself impatiently paging ahead as I read, looking for the next chapter break when I can leap up, run to the computer, and check for e-mail or the latest news on the Rialto. I'm not proud of this, but I must admit it's the current reality of my reading life.

It hasn't always been this way. There was a time when—as a kid—I could sit in an armchair in the living room for what, in retrospect, seems like uninterrupted hours without moving a muscle—except for the hand that turned the pages. I would be immobile for so long that, inevitably, my father would holler at me to go outside and play. What he didn't realize, of course, was that reading was play for me. Maybe that's a reason I just loved to read. It was fun; it was entertainment; it never occurred to me that what I was doing was "a difficult and complex art." Just as it never occurred to me that reading was also a—dare I say it?—learning experience. In reading, I was learning about the world around me; sometimes in factual detail if I was reading nonfiction, which I did avidly, especially biography and history. But I was also learning a larger, more amorphous reality about life, that it had both its joys and its sorrows. For a kid who had kind of a sucky life, the joys were especially welcome, suggesting, as they did, that life could be, well, beautiful.

As for those sorrows, I've never understood people who insist that every kid's book must have a happy ending. For the fact is that not every ending in real life is happy. On the contrary. Understand that I didn't like sad endings—I wept copious tears over the deaths of Old Yeller and Charlotte the spider and shook my figurative fist at their unfortunate fates—but I learned through reading that their endings reflected reality. And this helped equip me to assume, in due course, the role of adult in an uncertain world. Imagine the shock if I had only been exposed to happy endings, because I avidly believed in the reality of all the worlds I encountered in reading.

Oz was a real place to me, as was Freddy the Pig's Bean Farm, as was Narnia, as was Sherlock Holmes's gas-lit London. If I only concentrated hard enough, I believed, I could go to these places. And not only were the places real, but so were the characters who inhabited them. I think their vivid reality may be one reason why I learned empathy. I identified with these characters so intensely that when Freddy the Pig was afraid, and his tail came completely uncurled, I was afraid, too (even though I didn't have a curly tail). When the Wizard of Oz was revealed to be a humbug, I shared his shame. When Mole wept at the lost opportunity to go home, I cried copious tears, too. This acquired sense of empathy is the reason why today I can't pass a homeless person on the street without giving him money, even though I know it will probably be used to buy a bottle of booze. And yet I can't help but think, what if I were that person?

Yes, my heart (and my head?) is too soft, but I'd prefer that to having a heart that's too hard. If this means that, like Bill Clinton, I'll cry at the grand opening of a car wash, so be it. I worry about today's kids who are so consumed by the Internet, by social media, and by video games that they don't have the patience to read books, a reason, I believe, they are increasingly empathy-challenged. After all, who do they have to identify and sympathize with? A character in *Grand Theft Auto*?

I learned more than empathy from sustained reading, however; I also learned about right and wrong, I learned about the kind of person I wanted to be and maybe even how to become that person through emulation. I also learned about the kind of person I did not want to be, for which I say thanks to Captain Hook, Professor Moriarty, the Wicked Witch of the West, Shere Khan, and countless others.

In retrospect, I seem to have learned a lot of lessons from avid, uninterrupted reading. Even today, though my reading is, well, discontinuous, I continue to learn about the world from books and maybe more importantly,

I learn new lessons about the human heart. And any book which offers me that experience, regardless of its literary quality, is every bit as notable as those I read so uninterruptedly as a child.

March 15, 2014 • *Booklist*

Read and Discuss

YES, CLASS, THERE were book discussion groups before Oprah. In fact, some say the first book discussion group in America was founded in the seventeenth century by the Puritan religious leader Anne Hutchinson, whose group gathered to discuss religious tracts, which doesn't sound like much fun. Maybe that's why she then bade her group good-bye to found the state of Rhode Island.

Flash-forward, now, to the eighteenth century, and we have the literary salon, which flourished in Europe, especially in France, where the literary gatherings continued into the twentieth century, most notably in the one conducted in Paris by Gertrude Stein and Alice B. Toklas, the one, that is, where folks such as Ernest Hemingway and Pablo Picasso were fixtures. But I'm ahead of myself. Let's go back to the nineteenth century and 1878 to the founding of the Chautauqua movement, formally known as the Chautauqua Literary and Scientific Circle. It spawned book discussion groups nationwide, some 10,000 by the end of the century. The most famous of the Chautauqua groups was founded in the 1870s on the banks of beautiful Lake Chautauqua in southwestern New York state.

I became familiar with this one in the 1950s, when I was working as a page at the Logansport–Cass County (IN) Public Library. Every summer, Miss Holmes, the city librarian, and Miss Holden, the county librarian, packed a picnic lunch and drove off to spend two weeks at Chautauqua. Since neither of the ladies was exactly a ton of fun, I was never moved to go there myself, although I drove past it several years ago and got a speeding ticket for my trouble. But I digress. Back to book discussion groups and, this time, to post-World War II America and the inception of the Great Books Movement, which began as part of the curriculum at Columbia University and the University of Chicago and, by the 1950s, had attracted more than 50,000 studious Americans, who regularly attended Great Books seminars, often held at the local public library. I confess I always confused the Great Books with the Five Foot Shelf of Books, fifty volumes of great literature selected by Harvard president Charles W. Eliot in post-Civil War America. I was familiar with this gallimaufry of great books, since my great-great uncle Chauncey M. Abbott owned a set, which, as a kid, I coveted. Alas, when Chauncey died, my uncle Frank unilaterally took possession of them. Of all sad words of tongue and pen, and so on . . .

Anyway, this brings us to the redoubtable Oprah and her book club, which began in 1996 and spawned countless formal and informal book discussion groups all across this great land of ours until 2011 and the end of Winfrey's TV show. Happily, it—the book club, not the TV show—rose again like the phoenix in 2012 as the Oprah Book Club 2.0.

Lastly in our brief survey of the history of the book club, we have the One Book, One Community movement, which got under way in 1996 in Seattle, courtesy of librarian Nancy Pearl. Thereafter, the National Endowment for the Arts—in the wake of its alarming 2004 report "Reading at Risk," which found reading to be, well, at risk—started its Big Read program, which selects communities across America and funds their programs. Some of the books that have been read as part of this program include the usual suspects; for example, *To Kill a Mockingbird, Fahrenheit 451, The Great Gatsby,* and so on.

All this has set me to wondering what books I'd discuss if I were to start a group of my own. For starters, they'd all be young adult books, of course. I'd probably begin with Robert Cormier's *The Chocolate War,* not only because it offers rich opportunities in itself but also because it invites ancillary discussion of its driving philosophy of determinism and of the work of Cormier's acknowledged mentor, Grahame Greene. Next I'd go for Francesca Lia Block's five-volume novel *Dangerous Angels* (the Weetzie Bat books). Again, the books themselves offer an ample field for discussion, but they also invite consideration of Imagist poetry, a heavy influence on Block's style. That, in turn, offers an invitation to look at Imagist poet Amy Lowell's work. Another aspect of Block's work, magic realism, would lead us, by extension, to the work of Gabriel García Márquez. And so forth. Once finished with Block, we might go on to British novelist Aidan Chambers's masterpiece, *This Is All,* the most in-depth character study of a teenage girl extant. This could lead us to another great literary portrait, Henry James's *The Portrait of a Lady,* which could lead us to the French Symbolist movement, and so, as Kurt Vonnegut used to say, it goes . . .

So what are the benefits of such programs? The NEA has the answer, identifying half-a-dozen bennies: (1) reading encourages higher education; (2) good reading skills improve the economy; (3) good readers have access to higher-paying jobs; (4) reading provides opportunities for job growth; (5) reading increases cultural and civic participation; and (6) reading encourages active citizenship.

I confess that I have never been part of a formal book discussion group—well, that's not quite true. For about twelve minutes, I was once part of an informal group that met to discuss the works of Shakespeare but quickly devolved into an opportunity to drink wine, eat canapés, and gossip, a danger that faces a lot of book groups, I gather, although one of the benefits of these groups that the NEA doesn't mention is companionship. Think, in this connection, of that famous book discussion group the Inklings, whose members included C. S. Lewis and J. R. R. Tolkien. What would it have been like to have been a fly on the wall when those guys got together? To find out, read the marvelous new book *The Fellowship: The Literary Lives of the Inklings,* by Philip and Carol Zaleski. Then, class, pour yourself a glass of wine and discuss!

December 15, 2015 • *Booklist*

2

BOOKS, BOOKS, BOOKS

On Collections and Collecting

I DIDN'T SET out to be a book collector. That I did is an accident of acquisition. Consider: When I was a kid, I was besotted by Freddy the Pig, the talking animal hero of a series of twenty-five children's books by the late, great Walter R. Brooks. I had discovered the books at the local public library but was discouraged to learn that the library didn't have the full set of Freddy books. What to do? Well, at the age of nine, I determined to buy the missing volumes, starting with *Freddy the Detective*. Buying that book turned me into a book acquirer, a reader who, from time to time, bought a book that had struck his fancy without any thought as to how it might fit into a carefully planned collection. It wasn't until I was a senior in college working part-time in the Rare Book Room of Northwestern University's Deering Library that I decided that systematic acquisition would be a swell hobby. And so, as you'll read in the columns that follow, a collector was born, one who—at his high-water mark—owned 15,000 books. These columns celebrate not only my adventures in collecting but my adventures in *moving* my collections, for I have changed residences twelve times in twenty years. Why so often? Have I been trying to stay one step ahead of the sheriff? Read the columns and find out.

The Accidental Book Collector

I DIDN'T PLAN to become a book collector, you know. That I did is almost accidental and largely due to the Freddy the Pig books. For if the Logansport Public Library had owned the entire Freddy series when I was a kid, I might never have been infected by what Nicholas Brisbanes calls the "gentle madness." But since, for some unfathomable reason, the local library *didn't* have all the Freddys, I—avid reader that I was—couldn't rest until I had acquired the fugitive few. I began with *Freddy the Detective*, which I ordered in 1950—with some help from my mother, since I was only nine at the time—from Kroch's & Brentano's bookstore in Chicago. This was the very first book I bought with my own money, and once it arrived in the mail and I had experienced the exquisite pleasure of opening the package, seeing the long-awaited book inside, and then removing it from the wrappings to touch it, smell it, admire it from every conceivable angle, and flip through its pages, I was well and truly hooked. Look out, bookstores—new, used, and antiquarian—there was suddenly a new collector on the loose.

Well . . . that's not quite true, at first anyway. To be honest, I wasn't a collector at the outset: I was only an acquirer. And all I was interested in acquiring were books in favorite series that were not available at the local library—not only the Freddy books but also the Oz books. And then came the Tarzan books. And then—well, soon there were too many to buy with only my own resources, so I started asking for books for my birthday and for Christmas. Not just any books, mind you, but books that were on my personal wish list, which I had painstakingly assembled by hanging out in the book departments of the Ayres and Bloch's department stores in Indianapolis, left there while my mother, sister, and grandmother shopped elsewhere in the stores. But that was fine with me. Take all day, ladies. I may have been left alone, but no man (or boy) is an island when he's surrounded by a sea of books—and is determined to make every last one of them his! To that end, I was careful to always have paper and pencil with me so I could busy myself with making those birthday and Christmas lists.

Unfortunately, we went to Indianapolis only several times a year, so I didn't have regular, unfettered access to bookstores until I went to college. There I discovered a Kroch's & Brentano's store in downtown Evanston, Illinois, only blocks from the Northwestern University campus. More importantly, I also discovered the world of used bookstores (be still my heart), guided in this quest by Mr. Olsen, the Deering Library's curator of rare books for whom I worked twenty hours per week. I still remember the day when, browsing in a used bookstore on Chicago's North Side, I found and bought first editions of L. Frank Baum's *Queen Xixi of Ix* and *The Enchanted Island of Yew* for something like five dollars apiece. When I showed them to Mr. O. the next day, I thought he was going to have a coronary. I don't remember precisely what he said, but it started, "Oh, my God!" The lesson I learned from this? One of the shadier—but sweeter—pleasures of book collecting is finding you have things that other collectors don't. Heh-heh.

From the above, it's obvious that by the time I was in college, I had discovered children's literature as one of my areas of specialization and, in the process, had transformed myself from an acquirer to a kind of collector. I say "kind of" because I was not yet systematic about my new hobby; instead, I was collecting in the spirit of that great Chicago bookman Vincent Starrett, cofounder of the Baker Street Irregulars and author of *The Private Life of Sherlock Holmes* as well as of one of the best books ever written about books: *Books Alive,* in which Starrett notes, "In its simplest and happiest form, it [book collecting] means only buying, when one can afford it, the books of the day that one happens to like best, and keeping them because it gives one pleasure to have them around." It was Starrett who also said, "When we are collecting books, we are collecting happiness." Now that's *my* kinda guy!

As a result of reading those words, I've tried over the years to collect the books that have made me happy, not the books that were regarded by others as "rare and collectible" or that in any way constituted an investment, though occasionally things I've acquired have appreciated in value. And occasionally I've spent more than I could afford to get a book that—like those early Freddy titles—I simply *had* to have. These have usually been the rarest titles from the collected works of my favorite authors or illustrators—people like, oh, to pick a name at random, Walter R. Brooks, people whose *entire* body of work I *must* have. Fortunately, there have been only a few of those: in addition to Brooks there's Kurt Wiese (he who illustrated the Freddy books—along with [gulp] about 400 others! Oh, my achin' wallet . . .), Robert Lawson, William Pene du Bois, Kenneth Grahame, Leon Garfield, and the adult authors Anthony Powell, John Cheever, and Gore Vidal. But, alas, I also collect in subject areas—books about books, picture books, poetry, humor, Americana, literary biography, and, since the early 1990s, young adult books, the area in which I probably most closely approximate a serious collector and the area in which I'm now most focused and systematic.

Oh, sure, all of this has kept me poor, especially since I gave up the day job in 1991. But so what? Some people may have money in the bank. But me? Like Vincent Starrett, I've got happiness on my bookshelves.

I think I have the better deal.

December 15, 2005 • *Booklist*

Hercules Had It Easy

BY RIGHTS, MOVING should have been the eighth labor of Hercules, but the demigod was so frazzled after hosing down those Augean stables that he had to delegate this most onerous task imaginable to us mere mortals. And so here I am up to my eyebrows in excelsior and strapping tape preparing for my twelfth move in twenty years (we southern Californians are a footloose lot). For me, the act of moving wouldn't be quite so laborious if it weren't for all those (expletive deleted) books. Collecting them—some 10,000 at last guesstimate—has been such a routine part of my life that I never questioned the wisdom of it until the last time my books and I moved—on January 17, 1994, at 4:31 in the morning. We hadn't planned that particular relocation; it happened naturally when the earth underneath us moved—seismically—and we had no choice but to go along for the ride. It was the day of the great Northridge earthquake in Los Angeles, of course. I was shaken awake by the force of the temblor and bounced around in my bed like a pea in a pan as I listened to the thunderous crashes of the building collapsing around me. Or so I thought—and since I was living on the tenth floor of a 12-story apartment building, such a disaster scenario was a logical surmise—but what I was actually hearing was the thunder of 17 of my 21 bookcases crashing to the floor and flinging the books they contained to the nether corners of the apartment—some of those corners being 20 feet away. To get out of bed when the shaking finally subsided, I had to climb over a pile of bookcases that, like toppled tombstones, had fallen at crazy angles atop each other. To actually get out of the apartment—something I wanted to do with the utmost, shall we say, dispatch—I had to wade through a sea of books that rose at some points as high as my knees. The careless urgency that drove me to the front door brought with it a viscerally vivid understanding of Sir Richard Burton's intriguing proclamation. "Needs must when the devil drives." On reflection, it also brought to mind the thought, "Some people have babies. I have books."

Obviously, I got out of the building safely, but I wasn't permitted back inside for nearly three hours, while I frantically wondered how many of my babies had been destroyed—and, worse, how many had been destroyed by my stepping on them while trying to escape the death trap that a few hours earlier I had called my home.

Miraculously, after three days of intense labor had restored order to the earthquake-induced chaos, I discovered that not a single book had been damaged. But something had changed. For the first time, I found myself questioning the wisdom of collecting so many books that I could have been buried alive under them and to wonder, as well, where on earth this passion for collecting had come from in the first place. If it is hereditary, I have to look no farther than the nearest bookshelf for someone to blame. There is the evidence in a set of Robert Louis Stevenson's collected works (the 1904 South Seas edition): a bookplate with neat printing announcing the volumes are from C. M. Abbott's private library. C. M. was my great-great uncle, and though his full name—Chauncey Morgan Abbott—was grand enough to have belonged to a banker or a robber baron, the man was, more prosaically, a bookkeeper for the Pennsylvania Railroad. And yet, because he was also an avid book collector, this profession (book keeper, get it?) was, no doubt, the more appropriate for him.

A lifelong bachelor, C. M. lived with his books for company on the second floor of a big old house on Pleasant Hill in my hometown, Logansport, Indiana. My paternal grandparents, whom I often visited, lived on the ground floor. Unfortunately, because C. M. died in 1946, when I was five, I have only one fragile memory of seeing him and none at all of ever seeing his book-filled apartment. After he died, his collections were dispersed among various family members along with the glass-fronted bookcases that had lined the walls of C. M.'s rooms. My maternal grandparents had one of these bookcases, and in it I first discovered Oscar Wilde's fairy tales, weeping copious tears over "The Selfish Giant" before I was old enough to comprehend the symbolism that is its subtext. Also in that bookcase were *The Adventures of Sherlock Holmes*—which I read as a boy—and W. Somerset Maugham's *Of Human Bondage* (which I didn't). We had our own C. M. bookcase at home, of course, and it finally wound up in my room; indeed, most of C.M.'s surviving stock finally found its way to me. As the only book collector in the family, I was its natural legatee. I don't know how old Chauncey was when he began buying books; he was born in 1872 and somewhere I have a bookkeeping textbook that he studied as a teenager, but aside from that, the earliest of his titles I own date from the mid-1890s. As for me, I bought my first book—*Freddy the Detective*—in 1950 when I was nine. Having grown up surrounded by Chauncey's books, it seemed the most natural thing in the world to begin acquiring my own. I also don't know how many books he ultimately acquired, but I suspect that I own far more than he did—too many to house, in fact, and that's why approximately half of my collection is in storage. Consigning much-loved books to that cold, dark, distant room is like sending children to an orphanage. And along with the earthquake, this emotionally seismic experience has finally made me wonder if it is worth it, after all. Should I get rid of all those books and get a life, instead? But—as C. M.'s were for him—so for me my books have been my life. And you know what? Since I began writing the column you're reading, I have finished moving again (a planned relocation, this time), and the thrill of opening the hundred-plus, carefully packed boxes I've brought with me and seeing, inside, familiar, much-loved books in my still-unfamiliar surroundings makes me feel immediately at home. And makes me realize, too, that no matter how many times I may move in the future, so long as I have my books, wherever I wind up will be home. For all of us who love books, home is not only where the heart is but where the books are, too, and that is one and the same happy place where it is always good to be.

April 15, 1995 • *Booklist*

Heap o' Books

YOU'LL SCARCELY BELIEVE this—heck, I scarcely believe it—but it's true: I've moved again, lock, stock, and (book) barrel. Only three years after I wrote a column ("Hercules Had It Easy") in which I pondered the peculiar, uh, *challenges* of moving when you're a compulsive book collector like me, I find myself pondering anew what an almighty can-do attitude such an undertaking demands. And what motivation could possibly be powerful enough to set it in motion.

Last time, you may recall, it was precisely that—*motion*—which provided the impetus. I was living in a tenth-floor apartment when the January 1994 Northridge earthquake that hit Los Angeles sent all of my bookcases and their treasured contents crashing to the floor. The books came through the experience more intact than I did; at least they stopped shaking once the earthquake subsided! Me—I didn't stop trembling until I had moved outta there into another apartment eight stories closer to the ground. Unfortunately, since it was a smaller unit, I had to confront the truly heartbreaking task of choosing which books I would consign to storage. I survived that experience, just as I survived the earthquake, but both were emotionally wrenching and both sparked a serious reexamination of my priorities.

After the earthquake, I found myself questioning the wisdom of owning so many books—I could have been buried under them—but decided, ultimately, that for me, it's not a heap o' livin' that makes a house a home but a heap o' books, instead.

Because the heap in my new apartment was so much smaller, however, I now found myself obsessing about all of those books that were gone to storage but couldn't be forgotten. They were out of sight, to be sure, but never out of mind. I even found myself with a recurring dream: in it, I discovered a door in my new home that I hadn't noticed before; when opened, it revealed a big room with floor-to-ceiling bookcases filled with all of the books that had been put into storage! The joy of renewing my acquaintance with these old friends was so keen it routinely woke me to a disappointing reality and the increasingly frustrating knowledge that—since every conceivable nook and cranny in my two-bedroom apartment that could accommodate books (including the kitchen cabinets) was already filled with them—I couldn't even acquire a new book without getting rid of an old one.

Something had to be done, but what? There was no way that I could afford—despite the princely sum I'm paid for writing this column—a place in Los Angeles big enough to house both me and my 10,000 books. What to do? Well, fate—like Dolly Levi—has a way of arranging things. After all, it must have been fate that made me decide to say good-bye to the television program I had been hosting because, once the decision was made, I realized that this was the only thing tying me to L.A. And it must also have been fate that sent me off for a visit to friends who live in Chico (a college town 77 miles north of Sacramento), for once there, I discovered that I could rent a four-bedroom house for the same price I was paying for my two-bedroom apartment in Studio City! After careful reflection—lasting about two minutes—I was on the phone getting bids from moving companies.

That was the good news. The bad news was the discovery that the cost of long-distance moves—unlike local ones—is based, in large part, on the weight of the objects being moved. Do you have any idea how much 280 boxes of books weigh? I don't either, but I do know it translates into $5,000!!

Happily, a friend who—unlike me—could accurately be described as capable volunteered a solution: if I would rent a moving van, he would fly to L.A., help me move my 130 boxes of books out of storage and into the van, and then drive it to Chico for me. This cut the cost of moving by almost half, though it did leave me with the task of packing the 130 boxes of books in my apartment, but the pleasure of watching professionals load them, my 21 bookcases, and my furniture onto a van, and then hitting the road for Chico more than made up for that relatively minor inconvenience.

A month has now passed, and I'm more or less moved in. But it wasn't until this week that I found myself actually living that recurring dream. That's because another capable friend has just helped me build floor-to-ceiling bookcases on all four walls of my big back bedroom. They're not going to win any design awards from *Architectural Digest,* but they're functional and, as I discovered yesterday, will accommodate the contents of more than thirty boxes of books—how many more I'll find out today when I finish the job.

Yesterday was the true emotional payoff for the labors of moving: it was the first time I was able to dip into the boxes from storage, some of which had been there since the move that preceded the move that preceded this most recent one. In other words, some of them had been locked away in that dark, lonesome room on the sixth floor of L.A. Security Storage for more than six years. Opening them up and being reunited with their contents was a powerfully emotional experience not unlike digging up buried treasure or opening Christmas presents—literally in the case of those boxes that contained my collection of books about Christmas.

I rediscovered books I had sorely missed (like *The Holly Tree and Other Christmas Stories* by Charles Dickens, illustrated by the incomparable Ernest H. Shepard), books I thought I had lost (like my copies of James Marshall's George and Martha books), and books—too numerous to mention—that I actually had forgotten I owned.

It's taken me twice as long as usual to write this column because I keep wandering away from the computer and into the bedroom to look at all those books and to pinch myself to see if I'm dreaming.

Ouch! I'm not. That I'm awake and the books are real explains the goofy grin on my face.

Still (he said, frowning), there are 101 unopened boxes of books in the garage and only a few empty shelves remaining. On the other hand, there are *lots* of kitchen cabinets and if I take the doors off all the closets, I figure I could put bookcases in them, and I really use only one of the two bathrooms. The tub would hold a lot of books. Maybe, just maybe, I can manage to make enough room, at last, for all of my books.

If not, well, I'll just have to move again.

But not for another three years.

May 15, 1998 • *Booklist*

Where I Get Those Ideas

"WHERE ON EARTH do you get the ideas for your column?" is a question a seasoned writer like me gets all the time. (The Truth in Column Writing Act of 2002 now demands that I explain that "seasoned" simply means "old" and "all the time" means "twice in the last ten years.") Anyhow, it's a question I like because it (a) gave me the idea for this column, and (b) suggests that at least two people in America think I have ideas. Not to mention that it's a lot better than the questions I really am asked all the time—questions like, "Have you always had that turkey neck?" or "Are you wearing that tie because you lost a bet?"

Yes, sir, I'd much rather be asked the question about the source of my ideas than about my neck and what's around it. Not that I have a clue where my ideas come from, mind you. Ideas just sort of pop up out of nowhere—like fish when you dynamite a lake. But occasionally, no matter how many sticks of explosives you toss in, nothing comes to the surface. What do you do then? Well, looking back over my columns of the last ten years, I've discovered that the strategy I have most often employed is one of desperation: I move!

Apparently, my imagination was running on empty last May, since that's when I up and moved again—for the fourth time in eleven years. Since I'm writing for *Booklist* and not *True Confessions*, I'll spare you an exhaustive analysis of the peculiar pathology that has made me so relentlessly peripatetic.

And besides, the real issue here, the thing that's the perpetual fly in the ointment of my moving so often, is the fact that I have too many books. More than 10,000 of them now. So many that I've started to think of my collections as The Blob. Remember that early Steve McQueen movie about this, well, pink blob thing that keeps growing and growing, consuming everything in its vicinity? That's my book collection, eating up every atom of available space in my life. And there's no getting away from the blob. All you can do is take it with you. Or call in the air force to nuke it.

Since the air force has been otherwise occupied lately, I've had to bite the bullet of reality (have you noticed my elegant use of figurative language in this column?) and figure out if there isn't a better way of handling the book blitz.

It's not as if I had a choice. Once I had decided to sell the four-bedroom house in Chico, so I could move to sunny San Diego, I discovered that all I could afford there was a two-bedroom condominium. Can you say "downsizing," boys and girls?

A further complication is my reluctant realization that I'm getting older and may not live forever. I know, I know; it's hard to imagine a world without me, but facts are facts, and the inevitable day is coming when you won't have Carte Blanche to kick around anymore. An even grimmer reality is that I won't be able to take my books with me. Saint Peter has made clear that even heaven doesn't have room for all of them. So what's a collector to do? Especially a collector whose heirs don't have any compelling interest in books (doesn't the irony of that just kill you?). Well, I suppose I could sell my collections or grant testamentary permission to my heirs to sell them once I'm gone. But fat chance of that. For the sad fact is that I've given so much of my life and my most essential self to putting together these collections (which, collectively, own my heart) that such a thought is unthinkable. So what I've decided to do, instead, is to bequeath them to a university where they will be kept intact and available to students and, I hope, lovers of literature for young readers long after Uncle Michael has gone to that Carnegie library in the sky. The institution I've chosen as the beneficiary is California State University, Fresno—not because I'm an alum, but because Fresno is the home of the newly established Arne Nixon Center for the Study of Children's Literature. And here's the personal connection: I'm a member of the center's advisory board. The telling of the whole story of the center and my connection to it will have to wait for a future column. For the moment, it's enough to say that I'm confident that the center, curator Angelica Carpenter, and the university librarian, Michael Gorman (with whom I share a birthday), will ensure a warm welcome for my stuff. I say "stuff" because my collections include not only 400 boxes of books (at last count) but also countless boxes and file cabinets filled with papers—not newspapers (though there are some of those) but personal papers related to my life as a librarian, author, editor, host of the author-interview program *In Print*, and erstwhile Freddy the Pig authority. It will be a while (quite a while, I selfishly hope) before the center gets everything. But the process is already under way, and 120 boxes of that "stuff" left in storage in Chico will soon be headed to Fresno. In the meantime, I have come to San Diego, along with the remaining 280 boxes of books (and enough papers to fill five filing cabinets and a groaning storage closet piled floor to ceiling with boxes). The books are all unpacked now and placed higgledy-piggledy (pace, Freddy) on the shelves of the 34 floor-to-ceiling bookcases that line the walls in every room of my condo.

It's starting to look—and feel—like home. But the best part is yet to come: because I was in a hurry to move in, I simply put books as they came out of boxes onto the nearest available shelf. Now I get to organize them! The pleasurable anticipation that thought generates is enough to make me positively giddy and, more compellingly, to suggest that the *real* reason I move so often is that it gives me an excuse to play with my books. What more can one ask, after all? For in my lifetime I've learned one incontestable truth: the only surefire and sovereign remedy for what ails you is holding a baby . . . and a book. I don't have any babies, alas, but books I have a'plenty. And my heart is, accordingly, at ease in a new place that it can call home.

September 15, 2003 • *Booklist*

Boxes Everywhere

THE BOXES ARE everywhere—200 of them crowd every nook and cranny of the three-bedroom house that is my new home. You can't move without crashing into a mini-ziggurat of cardboard boxes containing all of my books—well, all that remain of my books, since I've just moved *again*—and because this was an especially ambitious relocation (more about that in a moment), I've had to be relentless in whittling down my collections. After sending another seventy-five boxes to the Arne Nixon Center at Cal State Fresno, what remains constitutes a core of collectibles, sentimental favorites (yes, my Freddy the Pig books), and reference books that I use in my work of researching and writing. From a high-water mark of some 15,000 volumes, my collection has shrunk to its present size, which I estimate to be somewhere in the scrawny neighborhood of 7,000.

And speaking of neighborhoods: Where have I moved this time? The answer (wait for it) . . . is back home to Indiana.

"Are you crazy?" a clerk in my new neighborhood pharmacy asked—a bit indelicately, I thought—when I stopped by to refill a prescription and mentioned I was newly arrived from San Diego, which boasts the best weather in the United States.

"It snows here, you know," the bank clerk added, no more than an hour later when I stopped by to open an account and told her I'm a new transplant from America's self-styled "finest city."

Yes, I thought, and it sleets, and it freezes, and in the summertime it's boiling hot and so humid you can wring water out of the air. But needs must when the devil drives, and the needs this time are family responsibilities that must be honored. And besides, here in tree-filled southern Indiana (just a hop, skip, and a jump down the road from fabled Brown County and Indiana University), autumn is spectacularly beautiful, and springtime is often sublime, lamb-soft and flowering.

Yes, I said *southern* Indiana. For I've come home to the Hoosier State but not to my old hometown of Logansport. Instead, I'm now a resident of Columbus, which lies thirty-eight miles south of Indianapolis. Here is where my family lives—what's left of it, anyway. That would be my twin sister and brother-in-law, my niece, my nephew, their families, and, lastly, my ninety-year-old mother, who, for the last eight months, has been living with my sister and is now, since the move, living with me.

The one unsettling aspect of this (aside from what the neighbors will think of a 65-year-old single man living with his 90 year-old mother, but let's not go there) is something that just occurred to me yesterday as I was telling the movers where to put the boxes of books and the twenty-five free-standing bookcases that will ultimately house them. I was upstairs (I have a two-story house) in the room adjacent to my bedroom that will house my book-filled office. My mother was downstairs doing what she always does—reading, working a crossword puzzle, or watching TV. I wasn't consciously aware of thinking about this, but, clearly, my subconscious was having a field day, since I suddenly found myself thinking, "Oh, my God! I've become Chauncey!!" If you're a regular reader of this column, you'll know that Chauncey is, more formally, Chauncey Morgan Abbott, my late great-great uncle, who, like me, was a book collector. He lived on the second floor of my father's family home on Pleasant Hill in Logansport and was regarded in the family as a bit of an eccentric (let's face it: anybody who loved books was regarded by my family as an eccentric, especially by my grandma Cart who lived downstairs from Chauncey. And if you'd like to know more about Grandma and C. M., I suggest you read my novel *My Father's Scar.* I say no more.).

They say that history repeats itself but never, in my wildest imaginings, had it occurred to me that I would become a latter-day Chauncey or, in my case, "crazy-old-Uncle-Michael-who-lives-upstairs." What a world, what a world . . .

Well, it could be worse. Unlike Chauncey, I flatter myself that I have a good (by which I mean loving) relationship with my family, especially with my three great-nephews: my niece's sons, Rhett and Wyatt, and my nephew's son, Andrew. The boys are ten (Rhett) and six (Wyatt and Andrew). At this point, none of them shows much evidence of becoming a book lover, but crazy old Uncle Michael is working on that! In the meantime, it's going to be a joy simply watching them grow up.

Columbus, too, is a nice place to live. Though small (only 39,000 residents), it's within easy driving distance of Indianapolis, Louisville, and Cincinnati. And, as I mentioned, Indiana University is just a hop, skip, and a jump down the road—just past a burg named Gnaw Bone, in fact.

A prosperous small city that has maintained the historic character of its downtown area, Columbus is also celebrated for its architecture. Thanks to the beneficence of the late J. Irwin Miller, president of Cummins Diesel Engine, which is headquartered here in Columbus, the city is filled with buildings designed by celebrated, world-class architects. The public library, for example, is the work of I. M. Pei (as a bonus, a heroic sculpture by Henry Moore adorns the library's entrance); the local newspaper is housed in a building designed by Skidmore, Owings, and Merrill; there are schools and churches by Gunnar Birkerts; a downtown mall by Cesar Pelli; a bank by Eero Saarinen; a senior citizen apartment complex by Gwathmey Siegel and Associates; and much more. I almost feel as if I were back in Beverly Hills but with a Hoosier accent this time (my sister lives on Washington Street, which is pronounced "Warshington" hereabouts).

All this and 7,000 of my favorite books that I'll begin unpacking just as soon as I finish writing this column.

Yes, it definitely could be worse!

September 15, 2006 • *Booklist*

My Environment

Environment: "The circumstances or conditions
that surround one: surroundings."

—American Heritage Dictionary

NOT SURPRISINGLY, THE surroundings that this Spotlight on Sustainability issue (you say *sustainability,* I say *environment*) contemplates are those of the natural world: oceans, trees, weather, birds, animals, and so on. As for me, though, being no nature boy, my environment is the interior world of my house, and its oceans, trees, weather, birds, animals, and so on are the nearly 8,000 books that fill the 222 shelves of the 37 six-foot-tall, freestanding bookcases that line the walls there. Yes, if I step outside, I'm surrounded by the natural environment, one replete with creepy, crawly, slithery things (shudder), but when I'm inside, I'm surrounded by a more agreeable environment, one of the mind, as represented by the books that fill each room of the house.

When I was a kid, the Walt Disney Studio routinely released documentaries called "Nature's Half Acre," which focused—sometimes microscopically—on the natural world of Mr. and Mrs. John Doe's backyard. In that spirit, let's take a gander at the eight rooms that constitute my own "half acre."

We begin with the living room, which houses seven bookcases. They contain my collection of British children's and young adult books. Frankly, I had no idea that I owned so many books from across the pond, until I acquired the four newest of the bookcases and undertook a massive book-rearranging project. Nothing delights the heart of the erstwhile librarian more than organizing and categorizing books, so I'm elated to have at last all of the British volumes in one place, where I can beam at my collections of Kenneth Grahame, A. A. Milne, P. L. Travers, T. H. White, Aidan Chambers, David Almond, Diana Wynne Jones, and more. Much more. Hot dog!

From the living room, we go to the kitchen, where there are two double-shelved bookcases, both housing the latest young adult books that I use for my various and sundry lectures and presentations. But wait! There's more: the pantry is also filled with books; these, shelved three deep, are the adult books I've reviewed for *Booklist* since 2004.

From the kitchen, we descend two steps into the library, a cozy room with a fireplace and seven bookcases. One of these, like those in the kitchen, contains new young adult titles; the other six house adult books, many of them classics from Walter R. Brooks's collections; for example, G. K. Chesterton, Henry James, Andrew Lang, Dickens, and such. My own adult books are here, as well: Gore Vidal, Anthony Powell, John Cheever, Tolstoy, Robert Louis Stevenson, and more. The seventh bookcase is filled with books about books and book collecting that make for some of the best browsing in the house. Light the fireplace, curl up in one of the room's two comfy chairs, and enjoy.

Off the library is the more workaday laundry room. Only one bookcase there, and it contains new young adult titles and another shelf of adult books I've reviewed.

Upstairs are three bedrooms, all of which might, instead, be called libraries, since each is filled with books. The two front bedrooms that overlook the street contain two and nine bookcases, respectively. Three of these eleven contain literary criticism and histories of both children's and young adult literature. Two contain graphic novels, comics, and picture books, while the remaining six hold my core collection of young adult books, starting with S. E. Hinton and continuing to the present day and such stalwarts as Walter Dean Myers, Gary Paulsen, David Levithan, Adam Rapp, and the like. The closet off the larger of these two bedrooms contains multiple copies of books by me and also extensive runs of magazines like *Booklist, Horn Book, School Library Journal, VOYA,* the *ALAN Review,* and even a run of *St. Nicholas* magazine from the 1880s and 1890s.

The hallway to the third bedroom also contains a bookcase; this one is filled with short story and poetry collections.

The third bedroom boasts five bookcases. One of these contains books about young adult literature; a second contains what I call Americana; for example, tall tales, books about the American West, Indiana history and literature, folk songs, and so forth. A third contains fairy tales and folklore; a fourth, L. Frank Baum and books relating to Walter R. Brooks. The fifth is a bit of an anomaly: a so-called lawyer's bookcase with glass doors that open up to reveal my collections of Freddy the Pig books.

Off the master bedroom is a huge walk-in closet, large enough to be a separate room. There are built-in shelves here that contain books about religion (including a modest collection of books about angels and angelology) and miscellaneous others; for example, an extensive set of the works of Bret Harte; a more modest collection of titles by the American poet Donald Hall, antiquities, and duplicate Freddy and Oz books. More excitingly, this room will soon house three new bookcases (when my nephew gets around to assembling them, that is). Into them will go my large collection of LGBT (i.e., lesbian, gay, bisexual, and transgender) books—and, yes, there is something ironic about putting them into a closet (!), but it tickles me to bring them out of the closet whenever I want to read them or refer to them for a new book I'm working on with my collaborator, Professor Christine Jenkins of the University of Illinois. (Our first collaboration, *The Heart Has Its Reasons,* was published in 2006.)

And that, ladies and gentlemen, concludes our whirlwind tour. I hope you've enjoyed this introduction to my environment. Yes, the outside world has its charms. It's beautiful today, for example; it snowed last night, and the trees are frosted with the white stuff. Yet, though the outside may delight the eye, it's the inside that pleases the heart, the mind, and maybe even the soul.

I'll opt for the inside. How about you?

February 15, 2013 • *Booklist*

3

THAT WAS THEN, THIS IS . . . Young Adult Literature, Past, Present, and Future

IT WAS FATE that introduced me to young adult literature. You must understand that my first love was children's literature and had been since I was a child myself. And so I was, as the British say, gob-smacked on the day in 1988 when I received an unsolicited letter from YALSA (the Young Adult Library Services Association), or YASD as it was then known (Young Adult Services Division), inviting me to serve on its Best Books for Young Adults Committee. Me? What did I know about young adult literature? But, intrigued, I accepted the invitation, went to my first committee meeting and, whoa, Nellie, fell in love overnight and have been faithful to the form of young adult literature ever since. Anxious to learn more about my new love, I sat down in 1994 and wrote a book about it, *From Romance to Realism*, which is now in its third edition. It confirmed my suspicion that I am, at heart, a literary historian, which explains why six of the eight columns in this chapter are devoted to the history of young adult literature. A seventh is a memorial to a history-making young adult author, and the eighth salutes a historic occasion. The past is present.

Happy Anniversary

HAPPY ANNIVERSARY, OLD friend. You're doing great and looking fine. Yes, young adult literature, that lively and dynamic genre, is now celebrating its golden anniversary, having come into existence in that portentous year 1967. Or did it? Did it perhaps stealthily spring into being earlier? That's one of the many questions I'll be addressing as I spend this and my next five columns examining the genre, past, present, and prospective. Each column will deal with a decade: thus, this first one will examine the 1960s; the next, the '70s, and so forth, until we arrive at the present. So let's climb into Mr. Peabody's "Wayback machine" and begin.

There's no gainsaying the fact that most observers date the beginning of young adult literature to 1967 because that was the year that S. E. Hinton's modern classic, *The Outsiders,* was published. However, the great Margaret Alexander Edwards, patron saint of young adult librarians, once pronounced that instead it was with the 1936 publication of Helen Boylston's *Sue Barton, Student Nurse* that "the dawn of the modern teenage story came up like thunder." Edwards wisely recanted this somewhat benighted opinion when she later declared that "it was in 1942 that the new field of writing for teenagers became established." Why 1942? Because that was the year Maureen Daly's bellwether novel, *Seventeenth Summer,* was published, with its closely observed examination of its teenage protagonist Angie Morrow's summer of love.

I tremble to disagree with the redoubtable Mrs. Edwards, but I have to point out that *Seventeenth Summer* must be disqualified because it was published as an adult novel, as was another book that has often erroneously been identified as the first young adult novel: J. D. Salinger's *The Catcher in the Rye,* published in 1951. Both certainly influenced the novels for teens that succeeded them. *Seventeenth Summer* sparked a decade, the 1940s, of romance, while *The Catcher in the Rye* gave a brash, wry, and cynical first-person voice to a generation of young adult novels that would flourish in its wake. More about that in a moment, but first a nod to the 1940s and '50s, two decades of genre fiction—rampant, squeaky-clean romance for girls; and, for boys, science fiction, adventure, and sports—not yet young adult but, instead, "junior novels," as they were patronizingly called.

But then here came the 1960s, and the times they were a-changin', demanding attention to and divergence from the traditional literature for young readers. Jeannette Eyerly began focusing attention on social problems that were newly plaguing teens in her books, which presaged the rise of problem novels in the 1970s. Frank Bonham, in his *Durango Street* (1965), cast a jaundiced eye on gangs, while Nat Hentoff spotlighted the impact of music on young lives in his *Jazz Country* (1965), a book, however, that he himself said failed. "The reality of being young," he observed, "the tensions, the sensual yearnings and sometime satisfactions, the resentment against the educational lockstep that makes children fit the schools, the confusing recognition of their parents' hypocrisies and failures—all this is absent from most books for young readers."

But Hinton was about to change that. The eighteen-year-old from Tulsa, Oklahoma, raised her voice in concert with Hentoff's when she passionately wrote in the *New York Times,* "The authors of books for teenagers are still 15 years behind the times in the fiction they write; romance is still the most popular theme, with a horse-and-the-girl-who-loved-it coming in a close second. Nowhere is the drive-in social jungle mentioned. In short, where is the reality?" Not in what she called "the inane junk lining the teenage shelf of the library." Instead, it was to be found in the pages of her own groundbreaking novel, *The Outsiders,* a searing portrait of the urban mean-streets gang warfare world of her compelling characters Ponyboy, Sodapop, Darry, and Dallas. The book caught fire like the incendiary decade that sparked it, and in its sudden celebrity—arising in part from the novelty of the author's youth (she was only eighteen when the book was published)—began to usher in a new generation of novels of contemporary realism.

Hinton was not alone, however, in her nascent influence. Robert Lipsyte, in his gritty novel *The Contender,* published the same year as *The Outsiders,* joined Hinton in the campaign against the unreality and vapidity that had previously defined teen fiction. Presto—the young adult novel was born. Arguably the first novelist to be caught up in its wake was Paul Zindel, the Pulitzer Prize-winning dramatist, whose first novel, *The Pigman,* published in 1968, portrayed the lives of two disaffected teens, John and Lorraine, and their devastating impact on the life and death of Mr. Pignati, the eponymous pigman of the title. Zindel, a master of dialogue, resurrected the wry, wisecracking, first-person voice of Salinger's Holden Caulfield, a voice that also informed John Donovan's 1969 novel *I'll Get There; It Better Be Worth the Trip,* which introduced the previously taboo subject of homosexuality into the still-new world of young adult books. And speaking of taboos, Zindel tackled another one—abortion—in his 1969 novel *My Darling,*

My Hamburger. In the meantime, Hentoff had returned, acknowledging the agonizing era of the Vietnam War with his 1968 novel *I'm Really Dragged but Nothing Gets Me Down,* which explored the hotly topical issue of the military draft and the ethics of avoiding it.

Thus, from 1967 to 1969 a revolution had visited the previously staid world of fiction for teens. Suddenly, attention had to be paid to the realities of a world that was sometimes inhospitable to teen lives, that played out on mean streets, that spoke in the real-world voices of disaffected youth, that set the pattern for the literature of the next decade, and that presaged the dawn of the first golden age of young adult literature. But for that we must await the advent of the 1970s, the decade we'll examine in my next column. See you then.

January 1 and 15, 2017 • *Booklist*

The First Golden Age

WELCOME, READERS, TO the 1970s, once called by cultural observer Lucy Rollins "a joke decade, defined by shag carpet, pet rocks, streaking, polyester leisure suits and the thump-thump of Beethoven to a disco beat." Joke it may have been in part, but the decade was also, more seriously, the first golden age of young adult literature. If it seems odd to declare a golden age for a genre that, in 1970, was only three years old, it evidences, I think, the long-standing, increasingly urgent need for a literature that would give faces to real teens.

And so, when S. E. Hinton, Robert Lipsyte, and Paul Zindel launched such an age, they opened the floodgates to a pent-up wave of hard-edged novels of contemporary realism to be offered by a spate of gifted young authors who would become grand masters of the genre. Consider the roster of writers who launched their careers in the 1970s: Judy Blume (1970), M. E. Kerr (1972), Richard Peck (1972), Lois Duncan (1973—Duncan had actually started writing light romance in the 1960s, but it wasn't until the '70s that she began writing her signature novels of suspense); Robert Cormier (1974), Walter Dean Myers (1975), and Lois Lowry (1977). All of these writers went on to receive the prestigious Margaret A. Edwards Award for lifetime achievement in young adult literature.

Nevertheless, it is Cormier, I would argue, who remains the most important; indeed, I would go so far as to say he is the single most important writer in the history of the field, a writer whose work alone would constitute a golden age. With *The Chocolate War* (published in 1974), he introduced literary fiction into the young adult fold, a literature rooted, in his case, in the twin philosophies of determinism and naturalism. Large, impersonal, often evil forces are at work in his universe, acknowledging the darkness that often pervades lives, teenage and otherwise. Indeed, in his work he takes his readers into the very heart of darkness, turns the lights on, and shows them the bleak landscape there. Thus, he became arguably the first to trust young readers with the truth that not every ending is a happy one.

Such thematic richness opened up enormous possibilities for those who would follow him, as reality became more, well, real and young adult literature became a more vital literary force. This is evidenced, in part, by the 1973 decision of the Young Adult Library Services Association to allow young adult books onto its long-standing Best Books for Young Adults list, which previously had included only adult titles. The first three young adult titles to officially appear were Alice Childress's *A Hero Ain't Nothin' but a Sandwich,* Rosa Guy's *The Friends,* and Robert Newton Peck's *A Day No Pigs Would Die.*

One important book never made the list, however: Judy Blume's *Forever,* issued in 1975, a novel that approached Cormier's *Chocolate War* in its influence on work that would follow. *Forever* is, of course, about Sex, with a capital *S,* the first young adult novel—and, for years, the only one—to feature a scene of explicit sex (and a penis dubbed "Ralph," which has occasioned generations of smirks and giggles). Until Blume celebrated it, sex had been a virtually taboo subject in young adult literature, and when it did appear, always offscreen, it was typically punished with dire results, often unwanted pregnancies that bade fair to ruin young lives. What was revolutionary about *Forever* was not only its inclusion of explicit sex but also the fact that its actors, Katherine and Michael, enjoyed the act and paid no enduring price for their action—except the end of their relationship, the title *Forever* being ironic. Though ahead of its time and influential, as noted, the novel suffered from some didacticism.

The best celebration of love and sex would have to wait until the 1980s and the publication of Francesca Lia Block's *Weetzie Bat.* But I'm getting ahead of myself. Back to the 1970s and a less salutary trend that informed the decade: the rise of the problem novel; formula fiction, that is, in which societal problems became the tail that wagged the dog of the novel. Characterization and other literary elements took a back seat to the issue du jour, whether it was parental divorce, sex, abortion, drugs, or rock 'n' roll.

Jeanette Eyerly set the pattern for the problem novel with such 1960s books as *The Girl Inside* (drugs), *A Girl Like Me* (pregnancy), and *The World of Ellen March* (divorce). Eyerly continued to write well into the 1970s, even as her '60s novels remained widely read. If she established the pattern, others quickly began pushing its parameters, sometimes sensationally, as did one novel that was published in 1970, the very first year of the decade: it was *Go Ask Alice,* by that celebrated author Anonymous, the purportedly "authentic" real-life diary of a teenage girl whose being is destroyed by drug dependence. It was, of course, a novel, not a real-life diary, and it was co-authored by Beatrice Sparks and Linda Glovach. So over the top and lurid that it quickly became a bestseller (and has never gone out print, selling millions of copies since), it is unintentionally hilarious in its melodrama (like the equally cautionary movie *Reefer Madness*), and, though originally published for teens, it is today read principally by middle-school students.

If the decade opened with the lurid, it closed with the lucid, the literary likes of Cormier's *After the First Death*, Terry Davis's *Vision Quest*, Hinton's *Tex*, Norma Fox Mazer's *Up in Seth's Room*, and Walter Dean Myers's *The Young Landlords*. It was, in retrospect, a decade of dramatic tension, a push and pull between the authentic and the specious, between a literature of realism and one of quotidian problems. Which would win this tug of war? For answers, we turn to the decade of the 1980s, and my next column.

February 15, 2017 • *Booklist*

Romance Redux

THE YEARS FLY by, and suddenly it's the 1980s, widely called the "me" decade, a fact that had little impact on young adult literature, since—for teens—every decade is a me decade. But teens are also a dynamic lot and, yes, fickle, so change visited the literature nevertheless. Its earliest manifestation was the decline of the problem novel and the unlikely renaissance of the 1940s romance.

Why this should have been is moot; it may have had something to do with a trickle-down effect, for the previous decade had seen an explosion of adult romance fiction. It may have been an exercise in nostalgia; after all, a 1940s movie star and former host of the 1950s TV show *Death Valley Days* was now resident in the White House. Or it may simply have been that teens had endured a surfeit of problems and longed for a simpler, more benign world. Be that as it may, romance once again ruled the roost as it had in the 1940s; one major difference, however, was that while teens in the '40s looked for romance novels by their authors' names—Janet Lambert, Betty Cavanna, Rosamond du Jardin, and so on—it was series titles they searched for in the 1980s: Wildfire, Caprice, Sweet Dreams, and—far outpacing all the rest—the phenomenal Sweet Valley High. (By the end of the decade, there were 34 million copies of Sweet Valley High books in print, and in 1985, the first young adult novel ever to reach the *New York Times* best-seller list was *Perfect Summer,* a Sweet Valley High "super edition.")

While romance was on the rise, public and school library budgets were on the wane; the taxpayers were, er, revolting, and accordingly, institutional budgets were busily becoming the incredible shrinking man. Where could publishers look to market their product? Why, to the teens themselves, targeting them in the chain bookstores found in America's ubiquitous malls, the teens' home away from home. "There is a teenage consumer force out there, and the only way to reach them is to go where their action is," declared Beverly Horowitz, then editor in chief of Pacer Books, a new line of paperbacks, a format that became a hallmark of the decade. Indeed, it quickly became a fact of publishing that a book would no longer be issued in hardcover unless it promised fat prospective sales as a paperback a year or so later.

Meanwhile, as boy-girl romances remained epidemic, another kind of romance, involving same-sex love, began cautiously to emerge with the landmark 1982 publication of Nancy Garden's *Annie on My Mind*, the first gay romance—with a happy ending, no less. *Annie* sparked a flurry of LGBTQ fiction in its wake. Consider that throughout the entire decade of the 1970s only nine books with gay content were published (and in the 1960s, only a single one!). The number quadrupled to thirty-six in the 1980s, a modest total but an indication that a new genre was aborning.

Speaking of new genres, near the end of the decade, romance was joined in the lists by a new kid on the series block: horror. Christopher Pike's 1985 novel *Slumber Party* is generally regarded as being the progenitor of the form, but Pike must share the spotlight with R. L. Stine, whose *Blind Date* was published in 1987, a forerunner to his immensely popular Fear Street and Goosebumps series. Though different in story content, romance and horror shared something in common: their characters were almost all lily white, middle class, and suburban.

Fortunately, that was about to change, thanks to the effect of Congress's having passed amendments to the Immigration and Nationality Act in 1965 that placed a ceiling on immigration from European countries while raising it for the rest of the world. The result was a major change in immigration patterns as the number of immigrants from Asia and the West Indies increased dramatically. In the meantime, the 1980s had seen the largest wave of immigration since the nineteenth century: 8.9 million people entered the United States legally between 1980 and 1990, and another 3 million, illegally. Was there a literature to give faces to these new Americans and other people of color?

Well, yes and no. It was 1965, the same year as the amendments to the Immigration and Nationality Act, when educator Nancy Larrick published her seminal article "The All-White World of Children's Books," which found that of the 5,206 books for young readers published between 1962 and 1964, only 6.7 percent of them featured characters of color. Happily, that was about to improve. Thanks to Larrick's article and the burgeoning civil rights movement, a black literary renaissance got underway, and over the next decade, authentic African American characters began to appear for the first time in books for young readers.

But what about those immigrants? Their story is less salutary. Though their sheer numbers cried out for a literature by and about them, they continued to be notable by their absence. Asian faces, for example, remained invisible until the 1990s, as, largely, did those of Latino young people. Why? Well, there are a number of reasons: one is that there have never been sufficient editors of color working in publishing, and two is that the editors who were there didn't publish enough authors of color.

We'll return to the issue of multicultural literature soon. But before we examine that, it's time to turn our attention to the 1990s, dark days for young adult literature, as we will discover in my next month's column. See you then.

March 15, 2017 • *Booklist*

A Near-Death Experience—Young Adult Literature in the 1990s

IN OUR SURVEY of 50 Years of YA, we now arrive at the 1990s, and what's that I hear? Could it be the death knell of young adult literature? Could it possibly be that the erstwhile lively genre was coming perilously close to its expiration date in the early years of the decade? Alas, yes.

Rapidly declining sales led editor Linda Zuckerman, for one, to say, flatly, "I think young adult literature is dying." Industry observer Connie Epstein chimed in: "Some editors, marketing directors, and subsidiary-rights directors have been wondering whether the young adult novel is ready for burial." What on earth had happened? Well, there is no easy answer. It was partly about a shrinking market, for the teen population had been in decline for fifteen years, while institutional budgets were experiencing a corollary devolution. Meanwhile, the 1980s had seen the rise of the middle-school movement, and as a result, a new category of reader, ages 10 to 14, had emerged, to be assiduously courted by the newly rampant chain superstores; Barnes & Noble alone opened 105 such stores between 1989 and 1992. These stores had no separate young adult sections; instead, they shoveled anything labeled "Teen" into their children's departments, where no self-respecting young adult would tread. As a result of all this, the average age of "teen" protagonists in young adult books dropped precipitously from 16–18 to 12–14.

Yet another nail in the coffin of contemporary realistic young adult fiction was the fact that, as publisher George Nicholson put it, the chains would not buy a novel "with anything difficult in it." Ironically, given these nightmare facts and statistics, one of the only areas of traditional young adult literature still flourishing was horror! Christopher Pike and R. L. Stine, dubbed "the Beavis and Butthead of horror fiction" by a cynical journalist, boasted, respectively, 8 million and 7.6 million copies of their books in print in 1993. Meanwhile, love, sweet love also continued to flourish, with the increasingly racy likes of Sweet Valley High registering 81 million copies in print in 1994.

Aside from that, nada. Well, nearly nada. There were a few traditional hardcover titles still being printed, but they were typically issued in editions of a mere 1,000 copies. Why, one wondered, even bother? Misery me, right?

Uh, wrong, for at the twelfth hour, things began to change. Significantly, for starters, the teen population suddenly began to spike, growing 16.6 percent from 1990 to 2000, when it totaled a robust 32 million. Meanwhile, the whole-language movement began putting serious young adult literature into the secondary classroom, creating a new demand for it.

Significant, these facts, but not the whole story: credit for the restoration of young adult literature must also go to professional librarians and educators who gritted their teeth and simply refused to let the genre die. For starters, two significant YALSA programs sounded a cry for the restoration of the genre. One was a preconference preceding the 1994 ALA Annual Conference, in Miami Beach, which reminded participants of the splendid past of the genre and the need for a similar future; the second was a standing room-only 1996 program in New York titled "How Adult Is Young Adult?" that focused on the imperative need to restore young adult literature to its previous high school-age readership.

The professional literature added its voice to a nascent young adult renaissance: in 1993 the venerable *Horn Book* magazine added a new column, Patty Campbell's "The Sand in the Oyster," which focused on young adult literature. The next year, *Booklist* began to feature my own young adult-centric column, Carte Blanche. That same year, emerging young adult author Chris Lynch published an influential article in *School Library Journal* titled "Today's YA Writers: Pulling No Punches," which called for the return of realism to young adult fiction. This was followed by author and editor Marc Aronson's sprightly article "The Young Adult Novel Is Dead and Other Fairly Stupid Tales" and my own article, "Of Risk and Revelation." In 1996, the venerable Children's Literature Association turned its focus to young adult literature for the first time by devoting an entire issue of its quarterly journal to "Critical Theory and Young Adult Literature," while that fall, NCTE's Assembly on Literature for Adolescents (ALAN) dedicated its annual conference to the theme "Exploding the Canon," which argued for the wisdom of using more young adult books in the classroom. Later that year, two books appeared that continued to focus readers' attention on the imperative need for young adult literature: Don Gallo and Sarah Herz's *From Hinton to Hamlet* and my own history of young adult literature, *From Romance to Realism.*

Meanwhile, American society was taking note of the expanding teen population and creating a new youth culture rooted in teens' dramatically expanding role as consumers. In 1995, people between 13 and 19 spent $68.8 billion on personal items, including books. As a result, Barnes &

Noble in 1996 began opening separate, stand-alone teen sections in its multitudinous stores. As a result of all this frenzied activity, young adult literature by 1997 had rebounded with a vengeance, reemerging in a new, more sophisticated form targeted directly at teens in high school, young adult literature's original demographic. These new hyperrealistic, risk-taking titles were quickly dubbed "bleak books" and excited considerable controversy for their boundary-breaking contents, which ranged from pedophilia to insanity, from murder to rape, and from juvenile incarceration to serial slaying.

If this sounds like problem novels gone berserk, trust me, it wasn't. It was, instead, a new literature of naturalism that brought art to its examination of the increasingly perilous world of teens. It signaled that "young adult literature" was no longer an oxymoron; anxious to demonstrate that fact, the Young Adult Library Services Association created its landmark Michael L. Printz Award in 1999, a prize awarded to the best young adult book of the year, with *best* being defined solely in terms of literary merit. For its impact on the literature, we must, however, wait for our next column, which will focus on the twenty-first-century period known as the New Golden Age.

April 15, 2017 • *Booklist*

A New Golden Age—YA Literature in the First Decade of the 2000s

HISTORY WAS MADE in the year 2000 when the first Michael L. Printz Award was presented to Walter Dean Myers for his groundbreaking novel *Monster,* signaling that young adult books had come of age as literature. That it had also come of age as a commercial phenomenon was demonstrated by the creation, in 1999, of publishing's first two young adult imprints, Avon's Tempest and Simon & Schuster's Pulse. As young adult literature has continued to burgeon in the years since, at least twenty-five other imprints have joined them. With the dawn of the new millennium, young adult literature began evolving at a dizzying pace, spinning off a near surfeit of trends.

One of the first of these trends was launched with the publication in 2000 of Louise Rennison's *Angus, Thongs and Full-Frontal Snogging* and with it the arrival on our sunny shores of chick lit, inspired by the British adult novel *Bridget Jones's Diary.* Chick lit (oh, that phrase) quickly evolved into what was called mean-girl lit, epitomized by Cecily von Ziegesar's *Gossip Girl,* with its meretricious celebration of the lifestyles of rich and famous teens, so consumed by commercial and brand names that the *New York Times* headlined a story about it: "Poor Little Rich Girls Throbbing to Shop." To industry observers, the mean girls heralded another trend: the rise of book packagers, who created *Gossip Girl* and the spate of more or less racy romances that followed in its wake.

Interestingly, the mean girls weren't the only ones who were throbbing to shop: a record number of real-life teens were buying books, 35.6 million of them in 2001. This $1.5 billion industry proved the fait accompli fact of an enduring market shift from institutional to retail, a trend that had begun with the 1998 publication of, yes, *Harry Potter and the Sorcerer's Stone,* which proved to be one of the most noteworthy phenomena in the history of publishing. The superlatives it spawned are well known: record-setting first printings—3.8 million for *Harry Potter and the Goblet of Fire,* the largest first printing in the history of publishing—sales of more than 375 million copies, and translations into 65 languages, all of which, reportedly, made Harry's creator, J. K. Rowling, richer than the queen of England. Equally rich were the trends that Harry and his cohorts inspired: they turned boys into readers; they were the first to attract record numbers of adult readers to books for the young (more about that in my next column); they made series publishing de rigueur, along with the seeming imperative that every book match the Harrys in length (don't forget that three of the last four Potters exceeded 700 pages); and they single-handedly turned the first decade of the twenty-first century into one of fantasy and speculative fiction. Not bad for an English schoolboy and wizard manqué.

Suddenly, everyone in publishing was searching frantically for the next Harry Potter, and it was found in the unlikely precincts of vampires and werewolves, who populated the four-volume Twilight series, by Stephenie Meyer (volume 4, *Breaking Dawn*, sold 1.3 million copies in its first 24 hours of publication). Stupendous sales were not the only legacy of Twilight; it must be noted that it ushered in a near-decade-long spawn of paranormal romance. The next winner of the celebrity sweepstakes was not long in coming. It was heralded by the 2008 publication of Suzanne Collins's *Hunger Games*. Its many successes and that of its two subsequent volumes—65 million copies in sales, translations into 51 languages, and sales in 56 territories—sent publishers into raptures of ecstasy, as did the translation of all three series into the holy grail of publishing: successful motion pictures. More literarily, *The Hunger Games* introduced a lively trend in dystopian fiction epitomized by the likes of Cory Doctorow's *Little Brother*, Saci Lloyd's Carbon Diaries series, James Dashner's *The Maze Runner*, and so on. The dystopian, post-apocalyptic novel heralded a renaissance of science fiction as well, and spawned a mini-trend in steampunk, which spilled over into the next decade.

Not all of the decade was symbolized by the supernormal, however. In 2006 *Looking for Alaska*, the first novel by John Green (who was soon to become the teen whisperer), won the Printz Award and reminded readers of the roots of young adult literature in the fiction of contemporary realism, a fact that would become preeminent in the next decade.

Though fiction ruled the roost in the first decade of the 2000s, nonfiction began to emerge as a force to be reckoned with too, though it was a new kind of nonfiction, called narrative nonfiction, a form that, in short, borrowed the tools and techniques of fiction without compromising its roots in reality. Examples appeared as early as 2000, the year Marc Aronson's *Sir Walter Ralegh and the Quest for El Dorado* was published and went on to become the first winner of the Robert F. Sibert Medal, which is presented to the author of the most distinguished informational book for children. Other young adult examples would include James Cross Giblin's

The Life and Death of Adolf Hitler and Jack Gantos's autobiographical *Hole in My Life*.

While we're talking about nonfiction, we need to salute a poetry renaissance, highlighted by the novel in verse, which was presaged by the 1999 publication of Sonya Sones's *Stop Pretending* and later epitomized by the wildly popular work of Ellen Hopkins. Other poets whose work distinguished the form in the first decade of the twenty-first century would include Ron Koertge, Helen Frost, Nikki Grimes, and Stephanie Hemphill, whose *Your Own, Sylvia* received a Printz Honor Award.

The richness of all these trends and realities leads me to call the first decade of the twenty-first century a new golden age of young adult literature, one that continues, as we will see next month, into the next decade of the century.

May 15, 2017 • *Booklist*

The Present and the Prospective

IN THE YEAR 2010, the second decade of the twenty-first century arrived accompanied by an unprecedented number of young adult books. When I first became involved with the field, in the late 1980s, a good year for young adult literature saw the publication of 250 titles. Today it is more like 5,000 (some say 10,000), and sales are stratospheric, up 22.4 percent in 2014 alone. With numbers come trends, and the field is now chockablock with them. Let's examine a handful as we wrap up our coverage of young adult books, past, present, and prospective.

For starters, we must acknowledge the fact that an astonishing 65 percent of all young adult books are now being purchased by adults, who have discovered and fallen in love with the genre. My guess is they were first smitten by the movie adaptations of the Harry Potter, Twilight, Hunger Games, and Divergent series, then stuck around to read the book versions, and now are devotees of the written young adult word.

This brings us to another trend: the current one in crossover publishing, a function of the increasingly fuzzy line between young adult and adult books and, frankly, the increasingly fuzzy line between young adults and adults themselves, as societal changes and recent research show that young people's brains are not fully formed until age twenty-five or so. This has led some observers to posit the notion that people are now not adults until age twenty-six. This population of post-high school 19- to 25-year-olds—called "new adults" by some, "adultescents" or "kiddults" by others—constitutes a new market segment that publishers will surely attempt to reach. Some already are as young adult literature becomes increasingly more sophisticated, a fact suggested by the review media's age-range designation "Gr. 10–up," for the indeterminate "up" invites appeal to new adults, as do the increasing number of young adult books featuring protagonists of college age (think of titles like Rainbow Rowell's *Fan Girl* and Sara Zarr and Tara Altebrando's *Roomies*).

A large number of adult books now could have been published as young adult books had sales and marketing staffs not dictated that the books would be more profitable published as adult. This works both ways, though. Margo Rabb's *Cures for Heartbreak* was written as an adult novel but was published by Delacorte as a young adult book. Another trend—the persistence of series—is rooted in the Harry Potter books. Some observers are now saying, however, that long series are finally in decline; one editor recently told me he is now looking for submissions that promise no more than a two- or three-volume story arc, while others are pointing to the increase in stand-alone titles.

One Potter-inspired trend remains unabated, however: books of Brobdingnagian length. There was a time, twenty or so years ago, when it was an unwritten rule that young adult books could be no more than 250 pages in length. No more! Today we routinely see books that are 400 to 500 pages long. An unofficial new record in this regard has recently been set by the publication of Daniel Kraus's splendid two-volume novel, *The Death and Life of Zebulon Finch,* which weighs in at a mind-boggling 1,400-plus pages.

Another new trend is a decline in speculative fiction (science fiction appears to be an exception) and a corollary return to a literature of contemporary realism, thanks in large part to the wildly successful work of a single author, John Green. This former wunderkind may, at age thirty-nine, no longer be a "kind," but he is still some kind of "wunderful," his mastery of social media pointing a path to success for today's emerging young talent. Further encouraging such talent is a still-new award from the Young Adult Library Services Association, the William C. Morris YA Debut Award.

Another important award for beginning writers is the Coretta Scott King Award for new talent. Which brings us to the consideration of multicultural literature, a topic we haven't visited since the decade of the 1980s, in part because this literature has persistently been a kind of publishing stepchild, noticeable by its relative absence. Happily, this may be changing, thanks in part to a new organization called We Need Diverse Books (WNDB). Founded in 2014, the nonprofit volunteer organization, according to its mission statement, "advocates essential changes in the publishing industry to produce and promote literature that reflects and honors the lives of all young people." WNDB's increasingly vital program of activities includes the newly established Walter Award, named in honor of the late Walter Dean Myers, and the Walter Dean Myers grants to encourage emerging talent in the field.

Meanwhile, another literature of diversity that is finally coming into its own is that of LGBTQ literature. After existing in the shadows for decades, LGBTQ literature has finally emerged into the spotlight of activity and acceptance. Like the rest of the field, it is now remarkable for its sheer volume. Consider that from 2000 through 2009, a total of 256 titles were published in this area, while for the lesser period of 2010 through 2016, the number has already escalated to 437! That's six times the total published during the entire decade of the 1990s! Equally remarkable is the emergence of books with transgender characters, the hottest trend in LGBTQ publishing. Though only three books with intersex characters have been published to date, my guess is that this, too, is a trend aborning.

What of future trends? Well, as long as young adult literature remains profitable—and there's no sign that it will be anything but—the field will remain in many regards the same, only bigger and, one hopes, better. For young adult literature is an essential staple of the lives of young (and new) adults, giving faces to every teen and a literature that rises to meet their personal, psychological, and social needs. It's been quite a ride to get from 1967 to the present, but keep your seat belts fastened, folks; there's a long and winding road yet to come.

June 1 and 15, 2017 • *Booklist*

The Dream Becomes a Reality

THE DREAM FINALLY became a reality in San Antonio. It was Monday morning, January 17, at ALA's Midwinter Meeting, when the Young Adult Library Services Association's president, Jana Fine, announced that the winner of the very first Michael L. Printz Award was Walter Dean Myers's *Monster* (HarperCollins). Three honor titles were also announced. They were *Skellig* by David Almond (Delacorte), *Speak* by Laurie Halse Anderson (Farrar), and *Hard Love* by Ellen Wittlinger (Simon & Schuster).

It was an unforgettable, emotion-charged occasion, viewed through tears by many. Some were tears of triumph; others sprang from the wish that Mike Printz himself could have been present to bask in the glow of history being made in his name. Could he have been there, I know exactly what he would have said to the assembled crowd, who gave his name a rousing ovation: "Well, bless your hearts!" That's what he would have said.

And I'm also confident that he would himself have led a resounding cheer for chair Frances Bradburn and the members of the first Printz Award Committee: Maria A. Gentle, Donald J. Kenney, Judy T. Nelson, Adela S. Peskorz, Pat R. Scales, Karlan K. Sick, Roger Sutton, Hazel Yliniemi, and *Booklist*'s Hazel Rochman.

In my opinion, they did an exemplary job and set a high standard for subsequent committees to emulate. It is no easy task to select—from a wonderfully diverse field—the best young adult books of a year as rich as 1999, especially when "best" is being defined solely in terms of literary merit. But this committee triumphed, and its selections offer compelling evidence to those who, including myself, would make a case for young adult literature's being now in the midst of a second Golden Age. The first took place in the 1970s, of course, and was ushered in by the 1975 publication of Robert Cormier's first novel, *The Chocolate War,* which became an overnight classic.

Fittingly, Cormier had a new novel himself in 1999, *Frenchtown Summer,* which was a departure in form for him; it was his first novel in verse. And in *Monster,* Myers, an established grand master of young adult literature who, like Cormier, is the winner of a Margaret A. Edwards Award for lifetime achievement, has similarly demonstrated the courage to take significant creative risks. As those who have read it will know, *Monster* is an experiment in form and structure, a novel told, not in traditional narrative, but in the form of a journal and a screenplay, both being written by a sixteen-year-old,

Steve Harmon, who is on trial for his life, having been accused of complicity in a robbery/murder. The nontraditional structure proves to be an extraordinarily successful device in the sense that it gives this young man, who says, "I feel like I have walked into the middle of a movie," an opportunity for emotional distance by making himself a character in the screenplay he is writing about his experience. At the same time, however, in his journal he is able to vent his passionate perplexity at finding himself in circumstances that previously would have been unimaginable: "The best time to cry is at night. When the lights are out and someone is being beaten and screaming for help. That way even if you sniffle a little they won't hear you."

Not only is this book an extraordinary literary achievement, it offers further evidence that the treasured artifact, the book, is undergoing some dramatic changes in the way it is being written, designed, and published. Surely this is a response to the fact that today's kids are the offspring of a visual generation, and that before their imaginations can be engaged by the contents of a good book, their eyes must first be engaged by its look. Thus, *Monster* features a three-quarter wraparound dust jacket (i.e., the paper jacket is only three-quarters the size of the printed board covers; when the jacket is removed, a different image is revealed underneath). But the visual innovation doesn't stop there. Steve's hand-lettered journal is printed on gray paper, and the text is sprinkled with pictures. Thus, the book becomes a kind of scrapbook of opportunities for eye stimulation, but one that works coherently to examine a teenager's life-changing experience. The illustrations are by Myers's gifted son, Christopher, who won his second Caldecott Honor award this year for the picture book *Black Cat* (Scholastic).

One of the three honor titles, Ellen Wittlinger's *Hard Love,* is similarly distinguished by its visual departures, which feature the inclusion of pages from teen zines (those self-written, self-designed, self-published magazines that teens all over America are producing), handwritten letters and poems, pages from journals, and the like. The wonderful thing about the visual innovations these two books offer is that the eye-stopping elements are not gimmicks; they are organic, arising naturally from the stories the respective authors share with their readers. More importantly, *Hard Love* is a heart-stoppingly good novel, offering a tender examination of the ill-starred love of a boy named John for a girl named Marisol—ill-starred because Marisol is an avowed lesbian. Its large-hearted treatment of homosexuality offers reason for cautious optimism that this often-taboo topic will now be treated with more openness and artfulness in young adult literature.

The choice of *Skellig,* originally published in England, is significant because it demonstrates that the new Golden Age of young adult literature is not confined to the United States. Moreover, its selection is another tribute to the wisdom of the committee in looking beyond the publisher-designated age range, 8–12, which appears on the book's dust jacket. Though this haunting novel can be read by children for the sake of its story, the complexities of its metaphysical theme and its wonderfully artful, open-ended ambiguity definitely mark it as a young adult novel. *Skellig* was also named Top of the List winner for Youth Fiction by *Booklist*'s Books for Youth editors.

As for *Speak,* here is an astonishing debut novel that is also an arresting departure in form. Divided into four sections, commensurate with a school year's grading periods, the novel abandons the traditional presentation of story in the form of chapters. Instead, the outcast protagonist, Melinda, tells her story in the form of scenes, each introduced by an intriguing heading that may recall, for older readers, title cards from silent movies: "Hard Labor," "Our Lady of the Waiting Room," "Clash of the Titans," and so on. What has happened to Melinda emerges in bits and pieces, fragments of form, imperative paragraphs that begin to cohere into a unified whole that speaks volumes about contemporary teen life. For not only is this a wonderfully sustained exercise in voice—Melinda's darkly ironic, wry, and often sardonic attitude toward the world is amazingly well done—but it is also one of the most acutely observed examinations of the curious culture of high school, with its clans, cliques, and failures of meaningful communication, to appear in ages.

Clearly, each of these books is extraordinary in its own individual way, but each has in common with the others innovation, creative courage, unimpeachable style, and, in sum, literary excellence.

Forgive me now for daring to speak for Mike Printz, but at this point, I am absolutely sure he would be busily bestowing blessings on each individual committee member's heart. And, speaking for myself now, my congratulations, too, on a job so well and meticulously done!

March 15, 2000 • *Booklist*

A Modern Master

THE RECENT DEATH of Robert Cormier left the world of young adult literature both poorer and richer. Poorer because there will be no more books from this modern master (though he left a nearly finished manuscript that may be published posthumously). And richer because in his lifetime he created a body of work so incomparable that it is impossible to imagine young adult literature without it. Indeed, I believe it is because of Robert Cormier that we can dignify the genre with that very word *literature*. Consider that his courage in being the first to demonstrate—in *The Chocolate War*—that not every young adult novel must have a happy ending opened enormous thematic possibilities for writers who would follow in his wake. Consider, too, that he was a master of complex, multidimensional characterization, and he invited his readers to speculate about the role played, respectively, by free will and determinism in the lives of his characters. And consider, in this regard and in his literary exposition of such other religious themes as guilt, evil, and the dark night of the soul, that he operated in the great tradition of one of his literary heroes, British novelist Graham Greene.

Indeed, Cormier once told a British interviewer that he thought Greene's *The End of the Affair* was one of the greatest novels ever written. Like Greene a Roman Catholic writer, Cormier once observed that his religion had always been "both boon and burden." Boon in the sense, one supposes, that it gave him his great themes as a writer; burden in the sense, perhaps, that it made him "a creature of guilt"—as he acknowledged in his Margaret A. Edwards Award acceptance speech in 1991. It also led, surely, to many moments of painful creation—like the moment he described the first time I heard him speak, many years ago in Los Angeles, the moment when he realized what would be the inevitable fate of Kate, the bus driver in *After the First Death*. That realization, he said, moved him to tears. This says a lot, of course, about his own emotional involvement with his characters, but, in his invocation of the word *inevitable*, it also says a great deal about that interest in determinism. And it says even more, I think, about his respect for his readers. A lesser writer might have decided to temper Kate's fate to protect teens' sometimes tender sensibilities, but Cormier believed that his readers wanted to be challenged, that they desired, as he said in his 1998 Frances Clarke Sayers Lecture, "an invitation to think, to use their brain power, to ponder words on a page and, almost miraculously in this visual world, to actually reread these words."

"Growing up in a world without much tenderness in it," he continued, "they seem to be searching for verities." He was unafraid to give them verities, even if they were accompanied by darkness. Yet he never lost sight of his responsibility as a writer for young readers, a responsibility that, he said, "makes me pause as I sit at my old battered typewriter. Are my words provocative merely for effect or are they sincere and [here's that word again] inevitable?"

This concern for his readers was expressed not only in his words but also in his deeds. He was famously available to young readers, who, finding his phone number in the pages of *I Am the Cheese*, called him at sometimes, well . . . unusual hours. But he was never too busy to listen and to talk with them.

Last year when I was still traveling the country, teaching seminars in young adult literature, I began each lecture by book-talking Cormier's novel in verse, *Frenchtown Summer*. I did this for many reasons: first, the book lends itself beautifully to such a presentation, but moreover, I thought it was one of the most important books of 1999. I loved it as a reader for its exquisitely elegiac language, for its hauntingly simple imagery, for its emotional honesty, and for the insights it offers into Cormier's own life and art. And, of course, because it gave me a chance to tell my audiences what I believe with all of my heart, that Robert Cormier is the single most important writer in the whole history of young adult literature.

Something quite lovely came from that; virtually every day, during one of the breaks, one or more people from the audience would approach me to share a Robert Cormier story. And though the particulars varied from teller to teller, the essential substance remained the same: all of the stories were about his amazing kindness and the generosity of spirit he manifested in his dealings with young readers, teachers, librarians, and beginning writers. I hope he knew the depth of the gratitude that people felt toward him.

What he desired to express in his work came as naturally as breathing to him: sincerity and absolute honesty in his expression of ideas and emotions. But nevertheless, as a writer, he was also tough-minded and rigorous in the integrity of his thematic development and his convictions about young adult literature.

In a 1996 letter to me he wrote, "I've thought for such a long time that YA literature has been a stepchild of children's literature, often neglected and misunderstood, and often praised and criticized for the wrong reasons."

Though he would, I'm sure, be embarrassed to hear me say this, it was his own work that changed that.

As I observed in my introduction of him at the Sayers Lecture, "For all of the writers who have entered the field since he began his career and for those who will enter the field in the future, Robert Cormier has set a risk-taking and transforming example. He has made it possible to write true literature for young adults, and not only for young adults but for older readers who are also challenged and stimulated by the thematic richness, the artful plotting, and the complexity of characterization that are the hallmarks of his books. They are, indeed, classics."

It is ironic that Jerry Renault's final words in *The Chocolate War* are "Don't disturb the universe." For his creator, Robert Cormier, did dare to disturb the universe, and for the world of young adult literature, that has made all the difference.

Thank you, Robert Cormier.

December 15, 2000 • *Booklist*

4

WITH A GENRE HERE AND A GENRE THERE

Historical Fiction and Romance

I SUPPOSE SOME might say that historical fiction and romance make, er, strange bedfellows. But not me. After all, don't forget that epic works of historical fiction are often called "romances." Think here of tales of old when knights were bold. I loved books like that when I was a kid but, really, any kind of historical fiction fired my imagination. This explains, I think, why one of my all-time favorite authors is the historical novelist Leon Garfield. You'll find my tribute to him in the column I call "Only a Great Man." And romance? Meh. Not so much for me, but I salute it nevertheless for its prominent place in the evolution of young adult literature. Don't forget that my history of YA is titled *From Romance to Realism* for a reason. And for more about that, check out the column called "The Object(s) of Their Affection," which is, what else? A history of romance fiction! Enough said. To the columns, citizens!

Back Home Again

I'M SITTING IN the adult reading room of the Logansport–Cass County (Indiana) Public Library. It's a bright, unseasonably cold afternoon in early April, and I've come back to my hometown for a few days to visit my mother before driving over to Kent State University to deliver a speech.

As usual when I'm traveling, I've brought along a briefcase full of work that needs doing and a bag full of books that need reading.

The work and the reading come together in one of those books, a copy of Leon Garfield's Phoenix Award-winning historical novel *Smith*, one of a series of Garfield reissues launched by Farrar, Straus and Giroux in 2000. I've brought it along as a catalyst for the writing of this column about historical fiction.

One of my favorite novels by one of my favorite authors, *Smith* is a book I've read countless times over the years. It never fails to please, starting with one of the best opening paragraphs of any novel this side of another favorite historical tale from my past, Rafael Sabatini's *Scaramouche*, which begins, "He was born with a gift of laughter and a sense that the world was mad. And that was all his patrimony."

I can confirm the accuracy of that quotation, by the way, since I just strolled back into the fiction stacks and, sure enough, found there a 1923 "movie" edition of this novel of the French Revolution "illustrated with scenes from the photoplay of the Rex Ingram Production." (One of the glories of this library is that its stacks are filled with such forgotten treasures from the past.)

As for the Garfield title, it begins, "He was called Smith and was twelve years old. Which, in itself, was a marvel; for it seemed as if the smallpox, the consumption, brain-fever, jail-fever and even the hangman's rope had given him a wide berth for fear of catching something. Or else they weren't quick enough."

How could anyone read either of these first paragraphs and not fall head over heels in love with historical fiction? I know I did. I was smitten with Sabatini when I was in junior high school (in fact, I read the very edition of *Scaramouche* that I just discovered in the stacks). My infatuation with Sabatini led naturally to my reading of other giants of historical fiction such as Hugo, Dumas, and Dickens.

As for Garfield—since his first book, *Jack Holborn*, wasn't published until 1964, I didn't encounter him until I was an adult in my twenties. And yes, the first book by him that I read was, indeed, *Smith*, which was published in 1967, the year I got out of the army and returned to Logansport as its assistant library director. And, yes, I just walked into the children's stacks and there found the very copy of *Smith* that I read those thirty-odd years ago! An automated circulation system has replaced the old Gaylord charging system that we employed back in 1967, but the original book pocket and card remain in books from that period, and the book card for Smith still bears the telltale imprint of my old library card number, 12927. Who says you can't go home again?

Finding connections like this to my personal history whenever I come back to Logansport reminds me that I have always been haunted by the past. Maybe it's because I grew up in an old community that was first settled in 1828. History was everywhere. And still is. A sprinkling of antebellum residences, which were sights as familiar to my preteen eyes as the little prefabricated house that I grew up in, still remain in the oldest parts of town. In fact, if I look out the window to my right—the one that overlooks the library entrance on Broadway—I can see, a block away on Market Street, the white pillars of the Nelson mansion, one of the oldest and grandest of them all, the proverbial big white house on the hill that every kid of my generation dreamed of growing up to own.

When I was a boy, Indiana history was a required subject in elementary school (is it still, I wonder?), and names like George Rogers Clark, Tecumseh, the Prophet, and William Henry Harrison were as familiar to me as those of my own family. Miss Beatty, both my fourth- and fifth-grade teacher, read aloud to us novels of old Indiana—Edward Eggleston's *Hoosier Schoolmaster* and *Hoosier Schoolboy*, Gene Stratton *Porter's Girl of the Limberlost* and *Song of the Cardinal*, and—most important—Florance Taylor's *Towpath Andy*, which was about the mid-nineteenth-century Hoosier canal days and was set, in part, in Logansport, for my hometown was once a port on the Wabash and Erie Canal.

Walk five blocks northwest of the library where I'm sitting and you'll come to the Eel River and, on its southern bank, crumbling pilings and an abutment, the remains of an aqueduct that carried the canal across the Eel at this point. Walk three blocks north of there, and you'll come to my paternal grandparents' old house, which was built in the 1840s as a tavern, where weary canal travelers could find refreshment.

This is not historical fiction, of course, but historical fact. Yet, as one grows older, time and memory have a way of blurring the distinctions. And we become, increasingly, characters in the unfolding novels that are our lives. In my case, this "novel" is inexorably turning from a work of contemporary realism into one of historical fiction.

Coming home to Logansport and, especially, coming back to the library that I directed from 1967 through 1973 remind me of this seeming melding of fact and fiction. Such visits are increasingly like rereading the early chapters of a half-forgotten book. The past and the present, once so distinct, have blurred together. As for the future, forget about it. It doesn't exist here in a town that, like so many others in mid-America, is slowly fading away.

So much about my town has changed for the worse in the thirty years since I left that it makes me sad to contemplate it.

But the library remains much as I remember. Oh, there are new light fixtures; the building—formerly an inferno in the summer—has been air-conditioned; an addition is under construction; but the fine old oak furniture is the same; the central, supporting stacks remain and are filled with books that still have the imprint of my old library card number, and the same three words are still carved above the entrance.

"Free to All."

Inevitably the day will come—melancholy thought—when I will no longer have reason to return to my hometown. Then my connection with it will exist only in the past, and my early life will have been wholly transformed into a historical novel. But a novel that promises to have a happy ending. For there are new books in the stacks here, and some of them are written by me. As an author whose work is represented here and as its once-upon-a-time director, my name remains linked with the library's. And in a small way, my name and the life it implies will remain an indelible part of the institutional and civic history of my hometown here on the banks of the Wabash far away. To the history-besotted boy I once was, this is a deeply satisfying thought.

May 15, 2002 • *Booklist*

Nightmare

"HISTORY," JAMES JOYCE famously wrote, "is a nightmare from which I'm trying to awake."

And small wonder, says I, when you consider the wisdom of another quotation, this one from the British novelist Thomas Hardy, who said, "My argument is that War makes rattling good history; but Peace is poor reading."

This is good news for historians, I guess, since it means they have absolutely no shortage of material to retail, given the superabundance in the past of wars, rumors of wars, and such other nightmarish events as holocausts, inquisitions, soul-destroying poverty, rampant greed, children's crusades, and slavery—all the atrocities that the Scottish poet Robert Burns surely had in mind when he wrote, "Man's inhumanity to man makes countless thousands mourn."

So what does this have to do with young adult fiction? Consider that the first definition of the word *history* in my *American Heritage Dictionary* is "a narrative of events; a story." And then couple that with philosopher George Santayana's familiar observation that "those who cannot remember the past are condemned to repeat it."

Since I would rather put my eyes out with white-hot needles than repeat the past or, even worse, visit that experience on any young person of my acquaintance, I declare—a bit stridently—that we must have more stories about the past, more substantive, well-written, vividly realized stories presented in the form of, you guessed it, historical novels, so that young people might become acquainted with the perversities of the past lest they be forced to experience them firsthand (we need more good works of narrative historical nonfiction, too, of course, but the spotlight here is on fiction).

All of this is why it drives me wild to hear my friends in publishing argue that it is "difficult" nowadays to publish historical fiction. First of all, whoever said it's easy to do the right thing? Second of all—at the risk of sounding cynical—I give short shrift to this argument, since I suspect "difficult" means "unprofitable," which would be one of the same reasons why it has always been "difficult" to publish another essential category, multicultural fiction.

Speaking of repeating history: way back in the early 1990s, I started ranting and raving about the imperative need for more good realistic fiction—and by "good" I meant well-written, of course, but I also meant fiction that trusted kids with the truth and that dealt with realities we had been reluctant to share because of the kids' "tender sensibilities." But how, I argued, can we use literature to equip them to deal with the exigencies of adulthood if we continue to pretend that this is the best of all possible worlds and that life is a hunky-dory stroll in the park (so long as you stay off the grass)?

To my delight, a period followed in which there was a rise in the publishing of just such works of authentic realism. Of course, this excited a certain amount of controversy, and some folks (especially those writing in the mass media) wrung their hands over the advent of such "bleak" books. To all of them, I wanted to invoke my favorite quote from Joan Rivers, to wit: "Oh, grow up." But I restrained myself and for about five years, we experienced a kind of golden period of authentic, unsparing, but artful works of realistic fiction.

But then came the rush—stampede, really—to fantasy, to speculative fiction, to horror, to genre fiction, especially that which bended and blended (imagine rich mean girls wearing cloaks of invisibility while shopping in a mall staffed by vampires and zombies). And so much for realism.

Yes, I am much given to hyperbole, but I was taken aback several days ago when—for a webinar I'll be doing—I put together a list of notable novels (in terms of popularity as well as critical reception) of 2010 and of these early days of 2011. I came up with a total of 117 titles, of which 23 were realistic fiction and 7 were historical fiction. That's 30 titles all told, which is not bad, one thinks, until one (that'd be me) realizes that also means 87—or 75 percent—were genre fiction. Oh, joy . . .

OK, this is when I say that I have no particular animus toward genre fiction; some of it is exceptionally well done, but I do deplore the imbalance here—especially in the area of historical fiction (5.9 percent of the total).

Trends tend to come and go without one's always noticing, and I had been still presuming that historical fiction was a fairly healthy area of youth publishing, as it was not so many years ago. When I put together my best lists for 2000 and 2001, for example, I found that 21 of 61 and 27 of 65 titles, respectively, were historical fiction! And some of the most distinguished novels of the past decade or so have been works of historical fiction: Aidan Chambers's *Postcards from No Man's Land,* for example, and Jennifer Donnelly's *A Northern Light,* M. T. Anderson's *The Astonishing Life of Octavian Nothing,* and Markus Zusak's *The Book Thief,* not to mention last year's

Wicked Girls, by Stephanie Hemphill and—for a slightly younger audience—Kimberly Willis Holt's *The Water Seeker*, Margi Preus's *Heart of a Samurai*, and Rita Williams-Garcia's *One Crazy Summer*.

These last three suggest there is a livelier historical fiction market for middle-school readers than for older young adults. That's fine, but just as I felt we needed more mature realistic fiction for older young adults fifteen years ago, so now I feel we need for them, too, a more mature, sophisticated, and artful historical fiction, one that is honest about the realities of history.

If we don't provide it, I'd suggest we must be prepared to relive it—starting with high school. Horrible? I rest my case.

April 15, 2011 • *Booklist*

Only a Great Man

OSCAR WILDE ONCE said, "Anybody can make history, but only a great man can write it." Only a great man, eh? Then, ladies and gentlemen, I give you the great Leon Garfield! The author of some fifty children's and young adult books, almost all of them historical fiction, Garfield (1921–1996) was a fine storyteller whose exuberant novels—inspired by Henry Fielding, Charles Dickens, and Robert Louis Stevenson—remind us of the unrivaled pleasures of reading. A brilliant stylist, he was also a master of plot and, always, of atmosphere, his novels being filled with mystery and secrets, surprises, and some of the most intriguing characters since, yes, Dickens. The analogy is an apt one, for Garfield, in a tour de force of writing, completed Dickens's last, unfinished book, *The Mystery of Edwin Drood,* adding, seamlessly, 19 new chapters to Dickens's 22.

Though chiefly set in the eighteenth century, Garfield's novels, like the best historical fiction, are timeless in their thematic treatment of life and death, of good and evil, of light and dark, as well as in their capacity to delight, stimulate, and satisfy. A recurring theme in them is the search for identity: thus, *Devil in the Fog* is the story of an eighteenth-century boy who, growing up in a group of strolling players, is claimed as the long-lost heir to a dying nobleman. "I use the quest for identity," Garfield wrote, "because I have a passion for secrets and mystery. And the secret and mystery of another individual seems to me the only mystery one can unravel endlessly—and still be uncertain."

In addition to his incomparable historical fiction, Garfield, in collaboration with Edward Blishen, undertook the retelling of a number of Greek myths in *The God Beneath the Sea,* which won the 1970 Carnegie Medal. A sequel, *The Golden Shadow,* was published in 1973. Later, in 1985 and 1994, Garfield transformed twenty-one of Shakespeare's plays into narrative stories in the books *Shakespeare Stories* and *Shakespeare Stories II.*

From his first book, *Jack Holborn* (1964), Garfield hit the ground running; his second book, *Devil in the Fog* (1966), won the first Guardian Prize. In 1980 he won the prestigious Whitbread Award for his novel *John Diamond.* In 1987 his third novel, *Smith* (published in 1967), won the Children's Literature Association's Phoenix Award, presented annually to the best English-language children's book that did not win a major award when it was originally published two decades earlier.

In the context of today's fiction for young readers, Garfield's work is absolutely au courant in its quintessential crossover appeal, and indeed, his first novel, *Jack Holborn,* a pirate story that evoked the spirit of *Treasure Island,* was submitted to the publisher Constable as an adult novel. An insightful editor there saw a children's book in it, however, and that is how it was published. Of this, book critic Humphrey Carpenter has said, "Like all of Garfield's fiction, it cannot be classified as exclusively juvenile or adult." Garfield himself said, "Really, what I try to write is that old-fashioned thing, the family novel, accessible to the 12-year-old and readable by his elders."

Readable is the key word in that sentence. Garfield was a master stylist with a sui generis voice; once begun, his books are almost impossible to put down. Consider these opening sentences from his novel about Smith, the young street urchin and pickpocket: "He was called Smith and was 12 years old. Which, in itself, was a marvel; for it seemed as if the smallpox, the consumption, brain-fever, jail-fever and even the hangman's rope had given him a wide berth for fear of catching something. Or else they weren't quick enough. Smith had a turn of speed that was remarkable and a neatness in nipping down an alley or vanishing in a court that had to be seen to be believed. Not that it was often seen, for Smith was rather a sooty spirit of the violent and ramshackle Town, and inhabited the tumbledown mazes about fat St. Paul's like the subtle air itself."

As this excerpt demonstrates, not only was Garfield a master of atmosphere and setting but also an author who—again like Dickens—wrote sympathetically of the impoverished and downtrodden in novels that approach works of social realism in their depiction of the daily lives of lower-class English men and women.

A native of Brighton, England, Garfield attended Brighton Grammar School and then went on to study art at Regent Street Polytechnic, but was forced to drop out due to his family's want of funds. He subsequently served in the Royal Army Medical Corps during World War II. "My war service," he once wrote, "was distinguished by a steady adherence to the rank of private. Yet those marvelously boring five years did have moments on which I've drawn repeatedly." One of those more somber "moments" was his assignment disinterring concentration camp victims, an experience of evil that, as I've suggested, also found its way into his novels. After the war, he worked as a biochemical laboratory technician at the Whittington Hospital in Islington, writing part-time until he was successful enough to write full-time, beginning in 1966. He was elected a Fellow of the Royal Society of Literature in 1985 and died of cancer on June 2, 1996. What was his best book? For me it is *Smith,* but many critics choose his brilliant twelve-volume series of short novels about London apprentices in the eighteenth century. It would be ironic if these were his best, since Garfield was no apprentice himself but, instead, a master whose work, full of life, energy, adventure, and humor, lives on.

April 15, 2015 • *Booklist*

The Object(s) of Their Affection

SINCE I HAVE about as much soul as a turnip, it's no surprise that romance fiction has remained pretty far off my reader's radar, even though I'm quick to acknowledge the historic importance of the genre to the evolution of young adult literature. After all, some would argue that the very first young adult novel was a romance, Maureen Daly's sweetly innocent *Seventeenth Summer*, which was published way back in 1942. Thanks to its pioneering example, the several decades that followed were chock-a-block with fluttering hearts and fragrant flowers, captured in the breathless, prom-celebrating prose of writers such as Janet Lambert, Betty Cavanna, and Rosamund Du Jardin, among others.

This remained pretty much the order of the day until the 1960s dawned and brought with them a bracing infusion of hard-edged realism, which, in its turn, then proceeded to rule the young adult roost for the next two decades. Ah, but romance is evergreen, and love is eternal—or maybe it's just that publishing is incurably cyclical; at any rate, then came the 1980s and a renaissance of romance fiction, expressed, this time, in an absolute explosion of original paperback series, though one name led all the rest, and, reader, it was Sweet Valley. Another decade later, after 106 Sweet Valleys had appeared, realism was ready to once again rear its ugly head—too ugly for some: remember the brouhaha over the "bleak book" phenomenon of the mid- to late 1990s? It didn't bother me all that much, but it is true that some of the brave new books that began appearing then made the hard-edged realism of the 1960s and '70s look like, well . . . Sweet Valley High! In the finest what-goes-around-comes-around tradition, the Sweet Valley series is now being reissued—with some fashion and technological tweaking, of course.

So I guess that brings us, more or less, to the present. And this is where it starts to get interesting. There are some, including me, who would argue that the catalyst for the rebirth of romance in the 1980s was a reaction against too much realism. Readers' appetites for unsparing looks at the real world had become sated, and the result was a stampede back to unreality, as depicted in the pages of escape literature. So did the same thing happen again as we entered the first decade of the twenty-first century? For we are once again smack-dab in the middle of a rush to series romance.

Well, yes . . . and no. There is no question that we are once again up to our eyebrows in romance, but this time it's with a twist or two. For one thing, the girl protagonists are no longer in love with the boy next door. Instead, they've now lost their hearts to . . . vampires and designer labels (and not necessarily in that order). For this revoltin' development, we can thank Stephenie Meyer and Cecily von Ziegesar for giving us, respectively, the Twilight series and the Gossip Girls. I say *revoltin'*, but frankly, most of my umbrage is reserved for the more meretricious maundering of Ms. Ziegesar. Meyer's swooning for the undead is more traditionally escapist stuff, and, while not my personal cup of tea, it is part of a large and, I would argue, essentially harmless tradition about which I wrote here last year ("Everlasting Love"). Losing one's heart—and soul—not to vampires but, instead, to luggage, handbags, shoes, dresses, and other consumables seems to me to be much more alarming, though here again not everyone would agree.

Novelist Elizabeth Hand, for one, wrote a scathing review of Meyer's final Twilight novel, *Breaking Dawn*, in the August 10 *Washington Post*, attacking the "distinctly queasy" male-female dynamic between vampire Edward, whom she perceives as a father figure, and klutzy, childlike Bella. Well, maybe, and where's Dr. Freud when you need him? But, nevertheless, if you must fall in love (and the heart does have its reasons that the mind cannot know), for goodness sake, let it be with another sentient being with whom you can walk, talk, smooch, and snuggle! After all, when's the last time you kissed your Manola Blahniks? (uh, don't answer that!).

There was a time (remember?) when young adult authors avoided brand names, knowing it would date their fiction. Now you can't read a page without your eyes literally falling over a brand name. Did you see the fascinating article by *New York Times* education columnist Michael Winerip that appeared on July 13? Headlined "In Novels for Girls, Fashion Trumps Romance," it quotes an academic study of the Gossip Girl books and two series they spawned—Clique and A-List—that found 1,553 brand names in their collective 1,431 pages. Even a mathematically challenged type like me knows that's more than one a page. It's not the girls, but the commercialism that's gone wild here.

But, then again, are these books truly romances? Well, maybe not in the traditional girl meets boy, girl loses boy, girl gets boy (and vice versa) sense. They may, more properly, belong under the rubric chick lit (or, in the case of Michele Serros's Honey Blond novels, chica lit), though whether that is a totally separate category or simply a hip and often self-mocking subgenre of romance, I'll leave it for you to say. (I pause here only long enough to remark that if the Bridget Jones and Georgia Nicholson books are paradigmatic examples, chick lit has a humor that is woefully missing from such shop-until-you-drop books as Gossip Girl, A-List, Clique, Sorority 101, The Celebutantes, The Au Pairs, The Ashleys, ad nauseam.)

Whatever you call it, this stuff is here to stay—for a while, at least. According to an article in the April 18 *USA Today,* "Youths are among the few categories of shoppers who seem comfortable spending freely these days." And I guess it could be worse. In a very funny column about the Twilight series, Gail Collins (*New York Times,* July 12) wrote, "Before you make fun of [the Twilight phenomenon], I want you to seriously consider whether you're interested in denigrating people who spend their leisure time actually reading books rather than watching *America's Got Talent.*"

Well, when you put it that way . . .

September 15, 2008 • *Booklist*

My Cicada Love Song

THE IRISH POET William Butler Yeats once famously wrote about living on the Lake Isle of Innisfree in a "bee-loud glade." Nice phrase, but if he really wanted loud, he should have come to my front yard and listened to the summer cicadas singing mating songs in the maple tree. It's enough to deafen you. (Fun fact: the cicada song actually is loud enough to cause permanent hearing loss if sung just outside your ear!) It's like hearing a bazillion lovesick human swains shouting, "I love you!" into their cell phones at a busy airport. Not exactly my idea of romance. But then I grew up when romance was quieter, a time when fellas still softly crooned "By the Light of the Silvery Moon" in the ears of their intendeds. (Fun fact no. 2: the 1953 musical comedy *By the Light of the Silvery Moon*, starring Doris Day and Gordon MacRae, was based on Hoosier author Booth Tarkington's Penrod stories!) Or if crooning failed, there was always the time-honored invitation to come upstairs and see your etchings.

I never completely understood that part about the etchings; I mean, I have etchings, for goodness' sake, and they are upstairs, but they're from Arthur Geisert's book *Pigs from A to Z,* and I don't find anything particularly romantic about them. But then I've never had a very deep understanding of romance. To this day, I don't comprehend the romantic appeal of a vampire or a werewolf or a pair of Manolo Blahnik shoes! But somebody does, since cross-species wooing is all the rage these days, not to mention losing one's heart to consumables (á la *Gossip Girl*). Was it ever thus? Well, yes and no. I don't think Manolo Blahniks were on the market in 1740 when the first romance, Samuel Richardson's *Pamela; or, Virtue Rewarded,* was published, nor seventy-three years later when Jane Austen's *Pride and Prejudice* appeared, though Austen's heroines were often spiffy dressers, and Lord knows, money and status were important to them. As for vampires or werewolves, don't look for them in the oeuvre of the Bronte sisters, who came along in Austen's wake, though *Jane Eyre* (1847) and *Wuthering Heights* (1847) both had a darkly gothic sensibility. (Fun fact no. 3: When I moved to California in 1973, I worked for a year in a Beverly Hills bookstore that carried a large inventory of series romances, most of which must have been gothics, since they all seemed to have the same cover art—a distraught young woman rushing away in terror from a forbidding-looking castle!)

Surely it's not too wide of the mark to say it was the Brontes who introduced what is now a hallmark of the romance novel: its genre-bending and -blending quality. Nowadays it seems that the only *pure* romance novels are contemporary series and contemporary single-title romances. Everything else is a sort of hybrid. Consider that the Romance Writers of America website lists seven of these hybrids: historical romance, inspirational romance, novels with strong romantic elements, paranormal romance, Regency romance, romantic suspense, and young adult romance. As for me, I'd add an eighth subgenre: GLBTQ romance, a type that started in 1982 with Nancy Garden's *Annie on My Mind,* the first gay novel to suggest that homosexuality is about more than sex; it's also about love! Hear, hear to that!

Anyway, despite the genre's long history, the modern romance doesn't seem to have really begun until the 1920s, when Georgette Heyer began writing her popular Regency romances; less than a decade later, the British publisher Mills and Boon began releasing hardcover romance novels. And in 1957 the Canadian publisher Harlequin started releasing these same books in the United States.

The next major benchmark didn't come along until 1972, when Avon published Kathleen Woodiwiss's *The Flame and the Flower,* and the thoroughly modern romance was born.

Thanks to the trickle-down theory of publishing, it was in the 1980s that it was finally young adult romances' turn to flourish. Most of these romances were, of course, original paperback series, scads of which contained the words *Sweet Valley* somewhere in their title. Or if not *Sweet Valley,* then *Wildfire, Sweet Dreams, Young Love, First Love,* and so on.

If the flame of romance fiction flickered a bit in the early 1990s, it once again burned with a gemlike intensity in 1998, thanks to the American publication of *Bridget Jones's Diary* by Helen Fielding, which had given birth in Britain to a new type of romance called chick lit. Though an adult title, *Bridget* inspired Louise Rennison's *Angus, Thongs and Full-Frontal Snogging,* which, published here in 2000, introduced chick lit to young adult readers. In due course, this new genre spawned (as in spawn of Satan) the mean-girl subgenre, which continues to flourish to this day.

Despite the existence of numerous romance subgenres, the experts at the Romance Writers of America stress that "two basic elements comprise every romance novel: a central love story and an emotionally satisfying and optimistic ending." Other than that, "romance novels may have any tone or style, be set in any place or time, and have varying degrees of sensuality—ranging from sweet to extremely hot."

And, I would add, they all have crossover appeal, which is to say young adults read adult romance, and adults read young adult romance.

September 15, 2011 • *Booklist*

5

OTHER WORLDS

Fantasy and Science Fiction

I WAS SURPRISED when I read my way through the 250+ columns I've written to discover how many were about fantasy and science fiction or, as they are now called, speculative fiction. I was surprised because I always think of myself as an exponent of and advocate for the literature of realism. But when I think about it, I realize how much of my early reading was devoted to works of fantasy, most notably, of course, the Freddy the Pig books (you'll find more about those in chapter 8). I suspect one reason why I've given significant attention to fantasy over the past two decades is because of its power to transport me into other worlds, far away from the vicissitudes of this too real one. Science fiction can offer the same experience, of course, but it has fewer charms for me because of its focus on, well, let's call it the technological and its cozy relationship with physics, neither of which is my cup o' tea. It's ironic, too, that for someone like me who wants to be transported to other worlds, science fiction now offers them too, all right, but they're all (shudder) dystopias. I'm not exactly a starry-eyed idealist, but I will acknowledge that given my druthers, I'd druther experience a utopia than a dystopia. Does Hogwarts qualify? Maybe you'll find the answer in the column I call "What Rowling Wrought." Speaking of escape . . .

Cutting My Teeth on Fantasy

AS A READER, I cut my teeth on fantasy. And I mean that both figuratively—in the sense that fantasy provided the stuff of most of my earliest independent reading—and literally, since I was in the habit of chewing on the covers and pages of my books as I read them. That would explain why my copy of a childhood favorite—*Raggedy Ann and Andy and the Camel with the Wrinkled Knees*—looks as if it had been the entrée at a termite picnic.

As a child, I didn't worry much about literary terminology (or the nutritional value of paper), so I wasn't aware that all of my favorite early books—Johnny Gruelle's Raggedys, Margot Austin's Peter Churchmouse series, Winnie the Pooh, the Freddy the Pig books, and a host of others—could have been described as fantasies of one sort or another. I only thought of them as being "make-believe," words that had a singularly sweet sound to my ears. Even then, I was aware that whatever these favorites were called, they shared one thing in common: they provided wonderfully genial alternative worlds into which I could escape from the vicissitudes of being—in the "real" world—a fat, smart boy who wore glasses and didn't like sports.

In retrospect, I guess it's fortunate that the neighborhood boys never caught me reading about Raggedy Ann, or I might not have survived to write this confession. Frankly, I'm a bit surprised myself that I so doted on Gruelle since I avoided all other "doll" books like the plague. What was his attraction? Certainly not the sentimental style: "It was very still and quiet in the play-house but the Raggedys were not even a teeny-weeny speck lonesome, for they were thinking so many nice kindly thoughts. And, you know, when one thinks only lovely, kindly thoughts there is no time to become lonesome."

No, it definitely wasn't the style. I suspect the attraction, instead, was his talent for pleasant invention and gentle humor—not unlike the talent that Howard R. Garis brought to Uncle Wiggily or Thornton W. Burgess brought to his Bedtime Story-Books, other childhood favorites of mine.

Unlike Garis and Burgess, though, Gruelle was also an illustrator who got his start in 1903 as a staff artist for the *Indianapolis Star* and went on to create a nationally syndicated comic strip, "Mr. Twee Deedle." His work as a children's book artist began in 1914 with an edition of Grimm's fairy tales. This was followed in 1918 by *Raggedy Ann Stories*, and the rest is literary history. Gruelle's pictures for the Raggedys and his other books are best described as, well . . . pretty in the way that Kate Greenaway's pictures were. And, in fact, his children are often dressed in the signature Greenaway Regency style. His animals are often clothed, too, but at least they have a good deal more character than the humans can claim.

And, happily, the style Gruelle brought to those animal characters derived not from Greenaway, but instead from W. W. Denslow (illustrator of *The Wizard of Oz*), from L. Leslie Brooke (*Johnny Crow's Garden*), and even from Randolph Caldecott (though without the master's signature wit and energy).

My favorite Gruelle book was not one of the Raggedys, which must have been a great relief to my father, but rather a stand-alone title, *The Magical Land of Noom*, published by Volland in 1922. This fantasy of a young brother and sister, Johnny and Janey, who build a flying machine and travel to the dark side of the Moon probably appealed to me because it is so reminiscent of the Oz books upon which I also doted. It even shared a similarly disappointing ending: after a bookful of wonderful adventures in a magical land, Johnny and Janey return home to the, ugh, real world just as Dorothy did in the first five Oz books. At least, she finally—in the *The Emerald City of Oz*, the sixth Oz book—had the good sense to remain somewhere over the rainbow.

Since I couldn't join her there, I was pleased to discover, as I grew older, that fantasy doesn't absolutely have to take place in an alternative world; it can also be set in our real one provided certain essential differences are stipulated. One of my favorites of these essential differences was that animals could talk. And, no, I'm not going to use this as an excuse to talk about Freddy the Pig except to acknowledge that his home on the Bean Farm was, indeed, the sty of my eye.

I also adored the world of Robert Lawson, especially *Rabbit Hill* and its wonderful sequel, *The Tough Winter*. Equally dear to my heart was his quartet of biographies by animals of the famous people in their lives—*Ben and Me*, *I Discover Columbus*, *Mr. Revere and I*, and *Captain Kidd's Cat*. Like Gruelle, Lawson was both author and illustrator, the first and only winner, in fact, of both the Newbery and Caldecott Medals. My favorite of all of Lawson's books, however, was not one of his children's titles but, rather, his only adult novel, *Mr. Wilmer*, which was published by Little, Brown in 1945.

It, too, was set in the real world—indeed, Mr. Wilmer's is the most quotidian of real worlds, drearily the same, day in and day out. Until the day of his twenty-ninth birthday, that is, when he discovers to his astonishment that he can converse with animals. This discovery, Lawson noted with dry understatement, "made a great difference in his life."

To a reader like me, this discovery provided the same shiver of satisfaction as did my recurring dream of one day waking up to discover that instead of Michael Cart I was, in reality, the slim, athletic king of a little known but strategically important Ruritanian kingdom somewhere in the Alps or the Carpathians, perhaps.

"I'm the King," I would then say grandly to my sixth-grade classmates, who had made my life a living hell with their teasing, "and you're nothin'."

A sweet dream, but if I had ever actually tried it, their reply would doubtless have been, "Then you're the king of nothin'."

Oh well, at least Mr. Wilmer got to live out his fantasy. And I got the vicarious pleasure of reading about it. Which is probably better than the real thing, anyway.

After all, who actually wants to sit around straining to make small talk with a hippopotamus?

April 15, 2002 • *Booklist*

What Rowling Has Wrought

WELL, DEAR ME. As if it weren't enough for the media to assert that Harry Potter's mother, J. K. Rowling, is richer than the queen of England; now here comes *Forbes* to put Rowling's name on its annual list of the world's richest billionaires (yes, that's billionaire with a b). Not too shabby for the author of five kids' books, eh? You don't suppose Rowling's unprecedented success has anything to do with the emergence of fantasy as one of the hottest genres in publishing for children and young adults, do you? And surely it doesn't have anything to do with the stampede of established adult authors to the suddenly oh-so-profitable young-readers' wing of the publishing industry.

This column will be about fantasy, but let's take twenty-two seconds (I timed it) to list the names of some of the established adult authors who are now also writing for kids. Let's see, there's Isabel Allende, Julia Alvarez, Clive Barker, Ron Carlson, Michael Chabon, Edwidge Danticat, Chitra Banerjee Divakaruni, Neil Gaiman, Carl Hiaasen, Alice Hoffman, Cynthia Kadohata, Elmore Leonard, Joyce Carol Oates, Francine Prose, and Ntozake Shange. Let's not even talk about the spate of celebrities who are "writing" picture books.

I'm not complaining, mind you, for it's all part of the rich pageant that is publishing these days, and anyway, some of the books that these authors are producing are actually very good. As for fantasy, well, it's positively flourishing in terms of both quantity and quality. And not all the credit—or blame—goes to the very wealthy Ms. Rowling; some of it is surely due to the singular success of a recent trilogy of movies about hobbits. Those would be the diminutive, hairy-footed ones who swept this year's Academy Awards.

The one-two publicity punch delivered by the Rowling-Tolkien combination has captured the imaginations of readers—and viewers—the world over, and the result has been a sudden renaissance of interest in a form that has been with us since Alice went down that rabbit hole in 1865.

Though fantasy has traditionally belonged to the world of children's literature—and to the ancillary adult world of sword-and-sorcery stuff with jacket art by the Brothers Hildebrand—it is also the quintessential crossover genre with inherent appeal to readers and dreamers of all ages. Certainly, Rowling's vast (and age-indeterminate) readership evidences this fact, but so too does the work of Philip Pullman, for don't forget that *The Amber*

Spyglass, the third volume in the His Dark Materials trilogy, recently became the first book for young readers ever to win the United Kingdom's prestigious Whitbread Award. Although Pullman's trilogy hasn't yet made it to the silver screen, an adaptation has found its way to the stage of Britain's National Theatre.

That said, however, a lot of the recent publishing activity in this field has been in the young adult arena. For proof, I just walked into the other room of my condo/home/office and, in a matter of minutes, found there sixty-eight young adult fantasy titles published between January 2003 and February 2004, and trust me, that's only the tip of the iceberg. What's amusing—and surely attributable to Tolkien and Rowling—is that almost all these books are either volume 1 of a forthcoming trilogy or part of a more extended series! The stand-alone fantasy seems to be an endangered species, although not altogether. After all, *The Tale of Despereaux,* Kate DiCamillo's delightful stand-alone, copped the Newbery this year, and more established masters such as Diana Wynne Jones, Margaret Mahy, and Terry Pratchett have continued to write marvelous individual tiles. Pratchett, of course, is also a master of the series form (his three-volume Bromeliad trilogy was reissued by HarperCollins in a single volume last year).

Many of these fine new fantasies are coming from England, where the form was born in the person of Alice (see above). Partly, this is thanks to British publishers such as The Chicken House, David Fickling, and Bloomsbury having recently established American presences. Another factor is the increasing globalization of publishing, which is bringing us more and more American editions of books first published abroad: Rowling leads this list, of course, but thanks are also due to Cornelia Funke from Germany (think Inkheart), Lene Kaaberbol from Denmark, Emily Rodda and Garth Nix from Australia, Kenneth Oppel from Canada, Catherine Fisher from Wales, and, well, the list goes on and on.

But American fantasy is also manifesting its own fecundity (God, I love alliteration!) in the form of newborn American imprints such as EOS from HarperCollins and Firebird from Penguin Putnam. As a result, the keepers—and generators—of the many annual "best" lists are starting to take notice. For example, two of YALSA's Top 10 Best Books for Young Adults last year were fantasies: Edith Pattou's *East* and Jonathan Stroud's *The Amulet of Samarkand* (the first volume of the Bartimaeus trilogy). And of the 84 titles on the basic Best Books for Young Adults list, 26 (that's a hefty 31 percent) could be described as fantasies—well, okay, as "speculative fiction," since a few of them border on science fiction—but that border has always been a bit blurry. If you doubt that, just ask the boundary-breaking dragon lady Anne McCaffrey, who recently won the Margaret A. Edwards Award for lifetime achievement in young adult literature. And to think that only a few years ago most fantasy junkies were griping that their genre got scant attention—and less respect—from the Best Books for Young Adults committee. My, how times have changed.

The teens themselves, of course, are devoted to fantasy. If you doubt that, check out YALSA's two newly established "Teens' Top 10 Lists." One of these is generated by YALSA's YA Galley Project (for more about this, visit the YALSA website); the other is produced by teens from all over the country voting via the Internet. Four titles appear on both lists, and three of these are speculative fiction: *Abhorsen* by Garth Nix; *Tithe: A Modern Faerie Tale* by Holly Black; and *The Thief Lord* by Cornelia Funke. As for the two individual lists cited above, 50 percent of the titles on both are fantasy.

As for the vast numbers of original paperback fantasy series, well, the mind boggles and reels. But then, come to think of it, that's what fantasy is supposed to do—boggle and reel the mind of the reader. Is it any wonder that scientists are now saying that the brain is a muscle that needs to be exercised? Well, so, too, is the imagination.

So, for heaven's sake, open a book and start flexing!

After all, your mind depends on it.

April 15, 2004 • *Booklist*

The Camelot Connection

IT'S SPRING AND, to paraphrase Tennyson, this young man's fancy has turned lightly to thoughts of . . . housecleaning! For me, this means hiring a latter-day Saint George to slay the evil dragon Grout that's taken over my bathroom tile. Meanwhile, I'm busy doing my part: cleaning up my files and dusting my bookshelves.

Rummaging in the stack of files, I happened on an article clipped from the November 5, 2005, *New York Times* headlined "Science and Religion Share Fascination in Things Unseen," by Lawrence M. Kraus. It contains the following paragraph, which I had highlighted on my first reading:

"It seems that humans are hard-wired to yearn for new realms well beyond the reach of our senses into which we can escape, if only with our minds. It is possible that we need to rely on such possibilities or the world of our experience would become intolerable."

Kraus may have been writing about religion, but has there ever been a more compelling argument for the importance of fantasy, science fiction, and that modern amalgam of the two that we've taken to calling "speculative fiction"? That is, books that specialize in "things unseen" and "new realms well beyond the reach of our senses."

Coincidentally, my rediscovery of this article comes on a day when I've been working my way through my collection of fairy tales and folklore. Frankly, I was never a big fan of either when I was a kid; I found Hans Christian Andersen depressing and thought the Brothers Grimm were downright scary, but this hasn't stopped me from assembling a wide-ranging collection of editions of their respective work along with half a dozen shelves of tales and lore from other hands (and lands). Poring over these books, I made an especially poignant discovery on the third shelf from the top: there was a long-neglected copy of a childhood favorite: Kenneth Grahame's *The Reluctant Dragon*, a wonderfully whimsical tale that first appeared as a chapter in the author's collection *Dream Days*. It's the story of a boy, an avid reader with a special fondness for natural history and fairy tales, who meets a dragon that is quite unlike the one that's laying waste to my modern-day plumbing. Grahame's is an affable, friendly dragon terrified by the prospect of having to duke it out with St. George. Of course, I had to take time off from dusting to reread the story, and, finishing it with a contented sigh, I placed it back on the shelf and then, on the next shelf down, my eyes fell on my rather ragtag collection of books about another knight in burnished armor, King Arthur.

Hot dog! I may not have cared much for fairy tales, but I absolutely adored the stories of the once and future king, his stalwart knights of the Round Table, and his shining court at Camelot. This was due, in large part, to my having discovered the Arthurian cycle not in the indecipherable words of Sir Thomas Malory ("Then were there no mo that durst be so hardy to set their hands thereto." Huh?) or in the poetry of Tennyson's *Idylls of the King* (what the heck were Idylls?), but instead in the four-volume retelling of author-artist Howard Pyle. Yet, even there, the lure wasn't the words but Pyle's amazing black-and-white drawings.

It wasn't until I was in high school that I finally found the version that completely captured my heart, my mind, and my imagination. It was, of course, T. H. White's incomparable *The Once and Future King,* his masterful reworking of his earlier four-volume novelization that included *The Sword in the Stone* (which I had discovered in junior-high school) and three additional volumes: *The Witch in the Wood, The Ill-Made Knight,* and *The Candle in the Wind.* Published in 1958 when I was a junior in high school, the resulting one-volume epic was, for me, an unforgettable reading experience.

My personal connection to White's great work goes beyond reading his words. For five years in the late 1960s and early '70s, my day job may have been director of the Logansport–Cass County (IN) Public Library, but my evenings (and weekends) belonged to the Logansport Civic Players. During that half-decade as an amateur actor, I played many parts, including Felix Unger in *The Odd Couple,* the title role in *Life with Father,* and many more. But the one I enjoyed the most, the one I think of as "the perfect part," was King Pellinore in *Camelot,* Lerner and Loewe's musical comedy version of *The Once and Future King.* Playing that part is the principal reason I decided to give up the day job and move to California in hopes of becoming a professional actor. One of the first parts I reprised when I got to Los Angeles was, you guessed it, King Pellinore. I don't know how many evenings I stood in the wings during the final scene, crying like a baby as I waited to go onstage. Because my cue to enter stage right was Arthur's singing the words, "Don't let it be forgot / That once there was a spot / For one brief shining moment that was known / As Camelot."

Call me an incurable romantic, but I believe that Camelot—the place, the musical, the *idea* that has so captured the imagination since Malory wrote about it in the fifteenth century—represents the perfect fantasy, the quintessential new realm into which we can escape.

In White's version, especially, there is a quality of innocent delight that is irresistible, but surely any version of the timeless legend proves there is no better place—to borrow another phrase from Lerner and Loewe—for "happily ever-aftering" than there in Camelot.

May 15, 2006 • *Booklist*

The Future Is Now

ACCORDING TO AN eye-catching headline in the *Washington Post,* "The Future Is Now." The story that followed, by one of the *Post*'s resident bloggers, Joel Achenbach, examined how technology—ever changing and ever more complex—is transforming the way we live. The trouble, it seems, is that we're not always aware of the changes or the engines that drive them. "Tomorrow's revolutionary technology may be in plain sight," Achenbach writes, "but everyone's eyes, clouded by conventional thinking, just can't detect it." Even smarty-pants scientists don't always recognize it, Achenbach asserts, concluding with the rather wistful question, "So where does that leave the rest of us?" His answer: "In technological Palookaville."

Well, welcome to my world, Mr. A. For when it comes to technology, I can out-Palooka just about anybody. In fact, my personal mantra for the last ten years has been "Thank God, I'm old and won't have to put up with this confusion much longer!"

But what's a befuddled columnist to do in the meantime? Well, if you're Achenbach, you turn for advice to Christine Peterson, who is vice president of the futuristically named Nanotech Institute in Menlo Park, California. Her recommendation? "Read science fiction, especially 'hard science fiction' that sticks rigorously to the scientifically possible. If you look into the long-term future and what you see looks like science fiction, it might be wrong. But if it doesn't look like science fiction, it's definitely wrong."

Well, OK, but that pretty much leaves me out, since I've always thought it was called "hard" science fiction because it's so blinkin' hard to comprehend. Or, if it's the cyberpunk variant, it's not only hard but also so hideously depressing that I'd rather not know what the future has in store—for me or for humankind, thank you very much.

I suspect I'm not alone in these disgruntled feelings, since contemporary science fiction of all sorts has definitely taken a back seat to fantasy in recent years. Oh, sure, this is partly due to the popularity of the Harry Potter books and the market forces they unleashed, but I do wonder if it might also be due to that dizzyingly accelerating pace of change I mentioned earlier and the technological complexities that change is visiting on the world. When reality is even more outrageous than imagination, there doesn't seem to be any compelling need for fiction, does there?

Good grief! What did I just say? Of course there will always be a need for fiction. Nevertheless, when one picks up the newspaper and finds speculation that the massive new particle accelerator called the Large Hadron Collider might, when activated, create a black hole that will swallow the earth, or that we can expect a billion-fold increase in information technology capability in the next twenty-five years, one does wonder just when it was that reality turned into fantasy, when the mundane became the marvelous. Maybe it was when the late Arthur C. Clarke first famously said that "any sufficiently advanced technology is indistinguishable from magic."

Well, whenever it was, it's no wonder that, as a result, the fairly sedate fictions we used to call science fiction and fantasy are themselves now morphing into something new that is increasingly being described by the umbrella term "speculative fiction"—a term that describes any work of the imagination that conjures up alternative realities, whether future or past, whether earthbound or set in other worlds.

What this fiction speculates about is becoming, it seems to me, ever and increasingly more . . . well, let's call it cosmic, as our knowledge of the universe continues to expand, thanks to space probes, orbiting telescopes, and whatnot. And if we are, indeed, going to be able to use such devices to peer far enough into deep space to witness the conditions of creation or to actually replicate them by using Large Hadron Colliders, then maybe science fiction needs to merge not only with fantasy but also with myth and metaphysics.

But, of course, it already has—in the work of Arthur C. Clarke himself. Such titles as *2001: A Space Odyssey; 2010: Odyssey Two;* and the earlier but still fascinating *Childhood's End* all speculate about such cosmic considerations. No surprise, then, that none other than C. S. Lewis hailed *Childhood's End,* saying, "There has been nothing like it for years." Not, perhaps, since Lewis's own Space Trilogy, which consisted of *Out of the Silent Planet, Perelandra,* and *That Hideous Strength.*

Such books presaged a marriage of high fantasy and science fiction that is now giving us such intriguing novels as Douglas Preston's recent *Blasphemy,* in which a team of scientists testing the world's largest supercollider find themselves engaged in a dialogue with God—or do they?

Clarke also featured a godlike entity in *Childhood's End,* one that he called "The Overmind," a kind of universal consciousness or intelligence with which a rapidly evolving humankind merged.

These large questions, which contemplate a new kind of humanity or new discoveries about the nature of creation and of reality (*Matrix*-like or otherwise), are the ones that fascinate me. I'm even willing to be interested—albeit grudgingly—in the possibility of the Technological Singularity that the mathematician and science fiction novelist Vernor Vinge (*Marooned in Real Time, A Fire upon the Deep,* etc.) posited some years ago. "It's possible," he argued, "that with technology we can, in the fairly near future, create or become creatures who surpass humans in every intellectual and creative dimension." To become, as it happens, the same kind of new humans that Clarke imagined evolving, though his did it without technology.

Still, whenever or even whether such things happen, I can't argue with Joel Achenbach, who concludes his *Post* piece by saying, "The future is going to be here sooner than we think. And it'll surprise us."

Fasten your seat belts.

May 15, 2008 • *Booklist*

The Possibility of the Impossible

IS THE WORLD really becoming a worse place to live in, or am I just growing older and more crotchety? I ask because I find myself once again fantasizing about escaping from this planet and the daily dreariness of living here. In last month's column, I was pondering the same thing, hypothesizing that historical fiction—the spotlight topic for that issue—had become trendy with teens because it offers a place, the past, of escape and refuge from the increasingly oppressive post-9/11 present. And now here I am, thinking the very same thing about fantasy fiction, one of the spotlight topics for this month's issue. But perhaps, in this latter case at least, such wistful speculation is unavoidable. After all, the creation of alternative worlds—even whole universes if the author is especially ambitious—is the stock-in-trade of many a fantasist. And a measure of the author's success in this regard is the verisimilitude he or she brings to the creation. Narnia, Middle Earth, and the Land of Oz, for example, are such triumphs of creative power that one wishes Lewis, Tolkien, and Baum might have been given a hand in the creation of what we laughingly (or despairingly) call the "real world." Surely they could have done a better job of it than—but I mustn't become blasphemous. It's OK, however, to muse a little bit about the presence here of such stuff as suffering, hatred, violence, intolerance, bigotry, gratuitous cruelty, pain, and all of the other things that invite us to echo Hamlet when he says, "What a piece of work is a man" (that would be only a few lines before he concludes, "Man delights not me").

This "problem of pain," as C. S. Lewis put it, surely invites consideration of the presence of both good and evil in human affairs, consideration that gives thematic weight to my favorite kind of fantasy, the kind the late critic Sheila Egoff, in her invaluable work *Thursday's Child,* called "epic or heroic fantasy," which, she goes on to explain, "is chiefly concerned with the unending battle between good and evil which is fought out in wide but well-defined landscapes." Usually these are the landscapes of alternative worlds of the sort that Lewis, Tolkien, and Susan Cooper, in her Dark Is Rising series, created to such stirring effect—usually, but perhaps not always. I think, for example, of the seven fantasies for adult readers that the late Charles Williams wrote. All of his titles, including *War in Heaven, Descent into Hell, Many Dimensions,* and *All Hallow's Eve,* are set in the real world that was contemporary to him (he lived from 1886 to 1945), but a real world that is regularly invaded by elements of the supernatural, for example, the holy grail appears in a country church in *War in Heaven*, and the Stone of Solomon shows up in *Many Dimensions*. Ghosts, adepts, and even the original Tarot make appearances in other of his volumes.

T. S. Eliot called Williams's books "supernatural thrillers because they explore the sacramental intersection of the physical with the spiritual." Like his friend Lewis, Williams was a Christian apologist and a member of that loose-knit literary society called The Inklings, to which Tolkien also belonged. The indefatigable Humphrey Carpenter wrote a fascinating book about these folks called *The Inklings* in the late 1970s, and it was this book that introduced me to Williams, whose novels I found simultaneously satisfying and terrifying. It is, after all, one thing to read about alternative worlds to which one must, somehow, travel; it is quite another to consider large and sometimes inimical forces invading our own real world. Reading this kind of book invites the reader to constantly look over his or her shoulder to see if, well . . . something might be materializing behind one's back.

Despite such frissons, I adored Williams's work, and I wonder if anyone still reads him in this country (there is a Charles Williams Society in England—see www.geocities.com/charles_wms_soc/). All of the novels appear to be in print in various editions, as is Williams's most celebrated work of theology, *The Descent of the Dove*, a history of the Holy Spirit in the church, a book that the poet W. H. Auden reread once a year, calling it Williams's "masterpiece."

The Inklings can't be mentioned without acknowledging the influence of the man Lewis once called his "master," the nineteenth-century Scottish fantasist and clergyman George MacDonald, whose many fantasies (*At the Back of the North Wind, The Princess and the Goblin, The Princess and Curdie,* etc.) are also informed by elements of the spiritual, the allegorical, and the mystical. It is not the mystical, though, but the "merely" magical that visits the real-world settings of another of my favorite fantasists, the Edwardian author E. (Edith) Nesbit, but this in no way diminishes her books' charm and, if anything, enhances their effortless humor. Who can forget *The Enchanted Castle,* or my favorite, *Five Children and It,* in which Cyril, Anthea, Robert, Jane, and their baby brother discover a strange, ill-tempered creature called the Psammead, who reluctantly agrees to grant them one wish a day. Of course, each wish goes hilariously wrong, as when Anthea wishes they were all "as beautiful as the day" (a lovely phrase!). Alas, when they are transformed, they discover that no one recognizes them, including the servants who refuse to let them in the house when they go home for lunch. "It was a horrible afternoon," Nesbit writes. "True, they were all as beautiful as the day, but that is poor comfort when you are as hungry as a hunter and as thirsty as a sponge."

For people like me who hunger and thirst for a world that is larger than what can be experienced by our five senses, fantasy will always have a powerful attraction. For it provides the possibility of finding the something more, the something that transcends the quotidian, the something that can be experienced only through the imagination, when it is properly fired, that is, by the visions of inspired writers such as Lewis, Tolkien, Williams, and the others who can offer us a tantalizing inkling of the possibility of the impossible.

May 15, 2007 • *Booklist*

The Possibilities of the Impossible

WHEN DIANA WYNNE JONES died on March 26 following a two-year-battle with cancer, the world lost one of its great contemporary fantasists. Jones, who was seventy-six at her death, was the author of more than four dozen brilliantly conceived and executed works of the imagination—or, in her case, make that a gloriously fertile imagination.

In its obituary, the *Guardian* observed, "Her intelligent and beautifully written fantasies are of seminal importance for their bridging of the gap between traditional children's fantasy as written by C. S. Lewis [with whom she studied at Oxford, as she did with Tolkien] or E. Nesbit, and the more politically and socially aware children's literature of the modern period where authors such as Jacqueline Wilson or Melvyn Burgess explicitly confront problems of divorce, drugs, and delinquency."

Jones's work, too, is not without its elements of darkness, but it is always infused with wit and wonderful invention as well. Mistaken identities are a hallmark of her books, and it sometimes seems that no one in them is ever who—or what—he or she at first appears to be. Similarly, her plots are complex, multilayered, and filled with surprises. Perhaps because she began her writing career as a playwright, her characters are so vivid and fully realized that they seem to live lives independent of the page.

Long before the advent of the more famous J. K. Rowling, Jones was producing her inimitable fantasies, many of which—like the Harry Potter novels—were titles in series, including the Chrestomanci series, the Derkholm series, the Dalemark Quartet, and the Castle series, one volume of which—*Howl's Moving Castle*—was turned into a splendid animated feature by the great Japanese filmmaker Hayao Miyazaki. Her stand-alone novel *Archer's Goon* (the first of her books that I read) was adapted for television in 1992.

Though some Jones fans felt it was a bit unfair that the younger Rowling should have had such extraordinary success and achieved a far greater degree of fame than Jones, it all worked out well in the end. For happily, when the Harry Potter books became an international sensation, publishers began frantically looking around for other books with the Potter appeal and there (ta-dah) was Diana Wynne Jones.

Thoroughly conversant with—and sometimes critical of—the time-honored conventions of fantasy fiction, Jones had great fun lampooning those conventions in her linked novels *Dark Lord of Derkholm* and *Year of the*

Griffin. Her lampooning is more straightforward in her *Tough Guide to Fantasyland.* The conceit of this droll exercise is that it is literally a tourist guidebook to Fantasyland. Entries are arranged alphabetically. Here are two typical examples:

"VAMPIRES are increasingly rare on the Tour. They have been attracted over to the Horror Tour by offers of better pay. Where they appear, you will find up-to-date Vampires who wear expensive sunglasses and wish to drain you of energy rather than blood."

"ZOMBIES. These are just the UNDEAD, except nastier, more pitiable, and generally easier to kill. When you slash your SWORD across their stomachs—which you will inevitably do—they watch their impossibly decayed intestines pour out in a glob, and then look at you with an expression of ultimate pathos before crumbling at the knees. Naturally they SMELL quite strongly."

Though not, as I've already mentioned, particularly well known in this country until late in her career, Jones nevertheless was the recipient of numerous prizes and awards; she was, for example, short-listed three times for England's prestigious Carnegie Medal. She won the Guardian Award, a World Fantasy Award for lifetime achievement, and an honorary doctor of letters degree from the University of Bristol. Three of her books have appeared on *Booklist*'s annual Top 10 Fantasy Books for Youth lists: *Dark Lord of Derkholm, Year of the Griffin,* and *Enchanted Glass.* One hopes these awards will further ensure that Jones *and* her work will be long remembered. Nothing magical about that: just simple justice.

Before I sat down to write this column, I reread *Enchanted Glass,* Jones's last book, and I'm very glad I did because it reconfirmed in my mind that Jones's creative powers remained at their lofty best to the very end. Like most of her work, it's very difficult to synopsize the plot of this one. Suffice to say that it involves a mild-mannered (well, sometimes) professor and a boy both beginning to realize their powers, a bossy housekeeper, a territorial gardener, a vegetarian giant, Oberon and Titania, an unlikely Puck, a weredog, and a village fete that goes very wrong, indeed. Typical Jones territory, in other words. And making it truly typical is its grounding in and deep respect for magic. Here is the professor, Andrew, deep in thought: "He knew that magic was one of the great forces of the universe that had come into being right at the beginning, along with gravity and the force that held atoms together, as strong as or stronger than any force there . . . it was a great power, to be used with great care."

In this case, the magic converges through two sets of enchanted glass and is best seen by both the boy and the professor when they remove their own glasses. I don't know if Jones wore glasses, but I do know she could see magic where the rest of us could see only the mundane.

The world will be a drearier place without her, but she leaves a wonderful body of work that will continue to remind us of the possibilities of the impossible. A richer legacy I can't imagine.

May 15, 2011 • *Booklist*

6

WHAT'S SO FUNNY?

Wit, Humor, and the Comics

MY FIRST BOOK—published in 1994—was titled *What's So Funny? Wit and Humor in American Children's Literature*. In researching it, I discovered a lot about humor, mostly about how useless it is to try to analyze this ineffable experience. Nevertheless, I give it a go in the column I call "Dissecting the Frog." As you'll see, I've coupled my love for humor with my love for comics in this chapter in part because comics used to be called "the funnies" (does anyone still call them that, I wonder?) and tickled our funny bones until we cried "uncle." My hat is off to all those who can give us the gift of laughter whether in text or in pictures, and I conclude this brief chapter with a salute to one of those gifted individuals, the great Sid Fleischman. He always left us laughing. Are there words of higher praise? I don't think so . . .

Dissecting the Frog

THE GREAT HUMORIST E. B. White once observed that "humor can be dissected as a frog can, but the thing dies in the process and the innards are discouraging to any but the pure scientific mind. Humor has a certain fragility," he continued, "an evasiveness which one had better respect. Essentially it is a complete mystery." Well, maybe, but it seems to me there are some clues strewn about that help us find the solution to who—or what—done it.

Maybe we should start by acknowledging that human beings are the only animal that laughs (though anthropomorphized animal characters in literature, like Freddy the Pig—you saw that coming—have been known to guffaw a time or two). We humans laugh, I'd suggest, in order to survive. Cumbered by a load of quotidian care, we find that a hearty laugh is liberating, a medicine for what ails us. If you doubt that, have a gander at Joseph Heller's and Norman Cousins's respective books *No Laughing Matter* and *Anatomy of an Illness as Perceived by the Patient,* in both of which the respective authors report on the therapeutic value of humor. Or hear psychologist Martha Wolfenstein, who has opined, "Joking is a gallant attempt to ward off the oppressive difficulties of life, a bit of humble heroism, which, for the moment that it succeeds, provides elation." Get out the party hats!

So what, to make life tolerable, do we laugh at? Well, Freud would tell us that we laugh at the forbidden, at what we fear, death being one powerful example. If you doubt that we can laugh in the face of oblivion, check out *Me and Earl and the Dying Girl,* Jesse Andrews's extraordinarily deft balance of glee and grief. As my colleague Daniel Kraus noted in his *Booklist* review, "This is one funny book."

Ironically, all of this talk of the funny is actually important, serious stuff, and yet humor remains the Rodney Dangerfield of literary forms: it gets no respect. Here's E. B. White again: "The world likes humor. But it treats it patronizingly. It decorates its serious artists with laurel and its wags with Brussels sprouts." This is why I was so pleasantly surprised when Louise Rennison's laugh-out-loud novel *Angus, Thongs and Full-Frontal Snogging* was crowned with laurels when it copped a Printz Honor Award. Also ironically, some observers, those who routinely complain that Printz titles are too literary to appeal to teen readers, also groused that *Angus* was too lighthearted to have been honored. Make up your minds, people! Happily, there was less dissension when Libba Bray's antic *Going Bovine* then won the Printz Award itself, or when Jack Gantos's exercise in self-deprecation, *Hole in My Life*, garnered a Printz Honor.

I hate to say it, but we humans do laugh at self-deprecation for a rather ignoble reason: we enjoy feeling superior to others. That merry madcap, the philosopher Thomas Hobbes, once said, "Sudden glory is the passion which maketh those grimaces called 'laughter.' It arises from a sudden conception of some eminency in ourselves, by comparison with the infirmity of others."

You may have noticed that I've now invoked the idea of irony twice. As this implies, irony—saying one thing while meaning another; for example, looking outside at a driving rainstorm and saying, "My, what a beautiful day"—is a staple form of humor, as is its twin, sarcasm. Another reliable form of humor, which might be called irony's cousin, is incongruity, the pairing of two generally accepted incompatibles; one of my favorite examples of this comes (again) from the Freddy books: it's found in the character of Leo the Lion, who has a penchant for getting permanent waves to keep his mane looking spiffy ("And I ought to have another permanent; there isn't hardly a crinkle left in the darn thing"). At the heart of the humor of irony and incongruity is another element: surprise. Marcel Gutwirth in his book *Laughing Matter* writes, "Wired for laughter from birth, we appear to have evolved this capacity to laugh from no other motive than a pleasurable surprise that serves no end but the enjoyment of our own momentary invulnerability in euphoria."

The forbidden, self-deprecation, irony, sarcasm, incongruity, surprise—what else makes us laugh? Well, how about exaggeration and eccentricity, especially when applied to character? Consider the pixilated, self-styled impresario Uncle Cornelius in Ben Tripp's *The Accidental Highwayman*, one of my favorite young adult books of 2014. "Before the door stood a thin, bent man with a white fringe of hair and white mustaches. He wore a soup-stained nightshirt and house-slippers. 'Great wheels of Parmesan cheese, is that young Myrtle?' the old man cried. 'Bless my barometer it's good to see you.'" And it's good for the reader to see him, for the eccentricities the elderly gent betrays are always good for a laugh, not least because of the inflated rhetoric he employs.

Of course, I've always been a fool for idiosyncratic voice, which is one reason why I so enjoyed Daniel Kraus's *The Death and Life of Zebulon Finch* and its protagonist narrator's use of what he calls his "flamboyant elocution," a hallmark of which is the polysyllabic. The voice isn't really intended as humor, but it invokes a feeling of delight, which humor at its best does.

The most satisfying humor is a kind of portmanteau contraption that incorporates a variety of elements. Ultimately, it is a playful way of looking at the world. As Beverly Cleary has noted, "Humor must spring from a writer's view of life."

Let us crown those writers with laurel wreaths or, what the heck, with brussels sprouts, too, for, really, wouldn't that be funnier than stuffy laurel? I think so. Ah, but what do I know? After all, I'm just a humble columnist with a penchant for the prolix.

February 15, 2016 • *Booklist*

Crazy about Comics

WHEN I WAS a kid, I was crazy about comics. Whatever the form or format: newspaper comic strips, single-panel cartoons in magazines, comic books—you name it; I was a devotee. I loved them all with a purple passion. Some of my happiest memories revolve around them. I remember haunting Shinabarger's Drug Store back home in Logansport, relishing the delicious sense of suspense as I waited breathlessly for that week's bundle of new comic books to arrive. Then there was the elation when it did, and I could pore over those new arrivals and decide which ones to buy with the dimes burning a hole in my pocket.

I also recall frosty mornings after I had spent the night at my grandparents' house—getting up early when the house was still quiet and bringing in from the front porch that morning's edition of the *Chicago Tribune,* the big-city newspaper to which Grandpa and Grandma subscribed. Of all the papers I had access to, the *Trib,* I would have argued, had far and away the best comic strips, *Little Orphan Annie* and *Dick Tracy* among them. As for magazines, there was the *Saturday Evening Post,* which, when it came to cartoons, was the poor man's *New Yorker,* with cartoons that I could actually "get" (Ted Key's *Hazel,* anyone?). So much did I love comics that I even read Munro Leaf's *Watchbird,* which appeared in my mother's copies of *Ladies' Home Journal;* that vaguely Orwellian comic featured "watchbirds" censoriously watching naughty children. Leaf also created the equally didactic *Manners Can Be Fun* and *Grammar Can Be Fun.* Fun? Says who? Of course, Leaf was also the co-creator, with Robert Lawson, of Ferdinand, the peace-loving bull, so all is forgiven.

Musing on this sort of stuff is an exercise in self-indulgent nostalgia, I suppose, but it underscores the impact of comic art on at least one kid and probably many, many more. It created in me what I might call a visual sensibility, an eye for the graphic and an appreciation for picture books and illustrated chapter books. I especially doted on those bearing the name Walt Disney: there was *School Days in Disneyville,* for example, and let's not forget *Donald Duck in South America.* Hot dog! But back to the comic strip. Aside from *Annie* and *Tracy,* what were some of my favorites? Well, there was Al Capp's *Li'l Abner,* with its annual Sadie Hawkins Day race (run, Abner, run) and *Fearless Fosdick,* its occasional parody of the hawk-nosed detective, who—in Capp's version—was routinely shot as full of holes as swiss cheese.

There was inarguably Charles Schulz's *Peanuts,* which debuted when I was nine (my mother said Charlie Brown reminded her of me!); and there were those other pesty kids, the Katzenjammers; the ineffable Pogo; the offbeat King Aroo; and, of course, the spinach-eating Popeye, who, in the beginning, was featured in a strip called *Thimble Theater.*

Then, of course, there were the great serial strips: *Flash Gordon, Terry and the Pirates, Steve Canyon, Prince Valiant, Mandrake the Magician, The Phantom,* and so many more. Just to say their names sends a pleasurable shiver up my spine. Sadly, there were great strips I missed, *Krazy Kat* chief among them. But there were also *Barnaby* and *Gasoline Alley.* Worse, the greatest of them all, *Calvin and Hobbes,* wasn't part of my childhood at all, since it didn't debut until 1985, when I was forty-four years old. But there were the comic books, the glorious comic books, the ur-graphic novels, that were a huge part of my childhood. I collected them as avidly as I did regular books. I kept mine in a box underneath my bed, not the best location as it turned out, since it was an invitation to an infestation of (ugh) silverfish. My favorite comic book was, of course, *Uncle Scrooge,* Carl Barks's pièce de résistance. (I recently discovered that Scrooge was one of graphic novelist Gene Luen Yang's favorites as well, so I was in good company.) Though a boy, I also doted on *Little Lulu* (hey, there were boy characters in it, too: Tubby, Iggy, Willie, and Eddie); this was the work of another great comic artist, John Stanley, whose work compares favorably with that of Barks, who was widely known as "the good artist."

Sadly missing from my comic-book collection were any superhero comics, since my mother decreed I could only buy "funny" books—that is, anything with the name Walt Disney on them, though I could also buy those featuring Bugs Bunny and, as mentioned, Little Lulu. Superheroes weren't altogether missing from my life, however, since I read their adventures on the sly at friends' houses. I liked Superman and Batman well enough, but my favorite was Captain Marvel, the alter ego of the newsboy Billy Batson, who transformed himself into the superhero by uttering the immortal word "Shazam." Interestingly, though Superman is by far the more famous, Captain Marvel comic books outsold those starring the super one in the 1940s. Aside from these big three superheroes, I also enjoyed the zany, sometimes surreal adventures of Jack Cole's Plastic Man, who could bend and stretch his body into every imaginable shape to foil the bad guys.

Unfortunately, the shape of newspaper comics these days is less than salutary, as shrinking newspaper budgets have dictated that the strips themselves be shrunk to a size so small that I have to use a magnifying glass to read the Sunday strips. And what a revoltin' development that is. Of course, I had to do the same with my favorite graphic novel of last year, *Nimona,* so perhaps it's not the comics and graphic novels that have diminished but my eyesight, instead. The joys of getting old. But no matter how old I get, one joy remains: memory's gift of nostalgia. Ah, good times . . . how I remember them.

March 15, 2016 • *Booklist*

Just Ducky, Thanks

I CAN SEE the headline now: "Duck Despoils Environment."

Come again? Does that even make sense? You bet it does when the duck in question is the world's richest and when . . . well, let's back up for a minute for some sorely needed context.

When I was a kid, I loved comic books with a purple passion, and among my hands-down favorites was the magazine called *Walt Disney's Comics and Stories*. How come? Because each issue led off with a ten-page story starring none other than Donald Duck, but not the one-note, jabbering, splenetic Donald of the movies; instead, he was a complex, multidimensional character who still lost his temper but was capable of myriad other emotions, as were his nephews, Huey, Dewey, and Louie, who were far more than the single-minded rapscallions of the movies. These kids were still mischievous but also smart—smart enough to routinely save their uncle when he inevitably went off the deep end.

I loved reading about their adventures, but most of all, I loved the episodes that included Donald's uncle Scrooge, the world's wealthiest duck. How wealthy was he? I thought you'd never ask. This guy possessed three cubic acres of money! His accountant reckoned that translated to 250 umtillion dollars and 16 cents. To put that into perspective, if Uncle Scrooge lost $1 billion dollars a minute, he'd be flat broke in 600 years. This guy was definitely a one-percenter!

When Uncle Scrooge made his first appearance in the 1947 Donald Duck story "Christmas on Bear Mountain," he was but a bit player. However, after he began to turn up in other adventures, he became so popular that, by 1952, he had earned his own comic called, simply, *Uncle Scrooge*. The first issue was titled, ironically, "Only a Poor Man." But that's not the one I want to put under the microscope this time; instead, let's take a gander at "Land of the Pygmy Indians," which appeared in June 1957. In it, we find Uncle Scrooge desperate to leave Duckburg with its chemical gases, smelter smoke, and factory fumes. "I'm through with it," he declares, "even though I am the guy that started all of those smelly industries. (Cough! Wheeze!)."

For Uncle Scrooge, to think is to act, and before you can say "malefactor of great wealth," he's bought a thousand lakes north of Lake Superior, a chunk of land measuring 200 square miles in area.

Enlisting the aid of his nephew, Donald, and his three great-nephews, Huey, Dewey, and Louie (whom he typically pays twenty-two cents a day for their labors), he's off to inspect his unspoiled property, with its myriad lakes that are clean and blue like sapphires and its air with its sparkling healthiness. It's a virtual paradise for an outdoorsman—er, outdoorsduck. And so Uncle Scrooge has brought along plenty of equipment for having fun hunting and fishing! But, alas, once a plutocrat, always a plutocrat; when his great-nephews innocently ask, "What do you intend to hunt?" his reply is "Gold, silver, nickel, copper. What else would a guy hunt?"

And so it begins. Everything the predatory duck sees is an opportunity: the timber can be turned into paper; the air can be bottled and sold; the moose can be turned into steaks that fetch two dollars a pound; an island might become a gas dome, where Scrooge could drill wells and pipe the product to chemical plants—"Oops!" says Uncle Scrooge, guiltily remembering what raw materials have done to Duckburg.

But how long will Scrooge be able to resist the limitless opportunities to make a buck? "He alone can decide that," his great-nephews declare.

Well, maybe not he alone, for as it turns out, this land is peopled by Native Americans, pygmy Indians who take strenuous exception to Scrooge's plans, no matter how tentative. They express their displeasure in verse with a meter that evokes Longfellow's "Hiawatha." Here's a sample: "We have caught the paleduck warriors // we have brought them to our council // brought them here to ask their reason // for their prowling through our waters."

After many a pinfeather-raising adventure, the ducks escape and return to Duckburg, where Uncle Scrooge says, "What is that wonderful smell?"

"Couldn't be the air," Donald says.

"It is the air!" Scrooge demurs. "The delightful aroma of the smelters! The perfume of the paper factories."

As I say, once a plutocrat . . .

When I was a kid, I had no idea who created these wonderful comics, for comic book author-artists then toiled in obscurity. The creator was known to his legions of fans simply as "the good artist." And good he was—a brilliant draftsman and an endlessly inventive author. Turns out his name was Carl Barks. Born on an Oregon grain ranch in 1901, Barks grew up to try his hand—unsuccessfully—at a bewildering variety of trades. "I was a fizzle," he wrote, "as a cowboy, a logger, a printing-press feeder, a steelworker, a carpenter, an animator, a chicken grower, and a barfly."

He's too modest about one of those enterprises: animator. For, though a self-taught artist, he was hired by the Walt Disney Studios in 1935 and assigned to work on the Donald Duck cartoons. He subsequently transferred to the story department, where he worked for six and a half years before he had an opportunity to illustrate a script for a Donald Duck story in *Walt Disney's Comics and Stories*. He fell in love with the medium, and the rest is history.

Barks's influence on other creative talent was widespread. Indeed, the scene in *Raiders of the Lost Ark* in which Indiana Jones flees before a giant boulder rolling after him was inspired by a similar scene in "Uncle Scrooge and the Seven Cities of Cibola."

Some years later, George Lucas himself penned an appreciation of Carl Barks in which he concluded of the stories, "They are a priceless part of our literary heritage."

To which I say, Amen, Mr. Lucas.

February 15, 2012 • *Booklist*

Magic Man

SID FLEISCHMAN CAME late to writing biography. He was already eighty-six when his first foray into the field, *Escape! The Story of the Great Houdini,* was published in 2006. Well, perhaps it wasn't technically the first, since he had already penned his autobiography, *The Abracadabra Kid: A Writer's Life,* in 1996 when he was just a kid of seventy-six.

Though Sid once told me, "Writer's lives are dull," his was anything but! A man of many talents, he began his career as a magician, traveling the country in the last days of vaudeville, but his interest in magic actually began when he was still in school and led to the publication of his first book when he was nineteen; titled *Between Cocktails,* it was a collection of tricks with paper matches "that could be done informally—between cocktails." Though Sid gave up full-time magic when vaudeville died, he never stopped performing tricks of magic and prestidigitation to the delight of adoring audiences of kids (and adults!).

After working briefly as a journalist, Sid began his writing career penning pulp mysteries; the first of these, *The Straw Donkey Case,* was published in 1948; another, *Shanghai Flame,* appeared in 1951; and still another, *Look Behind You Lady,* followed in 1952. Its protagonist was—you guessed it—a magician performing onstage in exotic Macao. Asian settings, by the way, came naturally to a man who had visited the East when he saw service in the navy during World War II.

Sid's varied career took another turn in 1955 when he became a successful Hollywood screenwriter, but finally, in 1962, he turned to children's books. His first effort, *Mr. Mysterious and Company,* was written, he often claimed, so his three children would understand why their father stayed home all day pecking at a typewriter. Interestingly, there was a similar motive behind the writing of his autobiography, which, he once told me, was penned "to let my kids know things about my life they hadn't heard before."

Over the course of the thirty or so years I knew him, I had many opportunities to hear him reminisce on such things, though he always preferred hearing what you were working on to talking about what he was doing. Many of these conversations came in the form of interviews I conducted with him. The last of these came in 2008 when an ALA conference in Anaheim brought us together for breakfast and a chance to talk about his newest endeavor, limning the lives of others. Naturally, I asked what had sparked this new venture, and he explained that writing his Holocaust-related novel, *The Entertainer and the Dybbuk*, had been a transformative experience, making it difficult to find subjects for future novels that didn't seem frivolous by comparison. And so, while he was casting about for ideas, he undertook writing a biography as "a welcome breather."

Choosing the subject of his first biography was a no-brainer; it had to be Harry Houdini, "the world's greatest magician." Writing a biography was, Sid said a bit ruefully, "like getting married—you only really get to know your subject after the marriage ceremony." And though his admiration for Houdini's talent was boundless, he found himself becoming increasingly fed up with the man's "colossal ego." Nevertheless, the finished work was a huge success, so much so that Sid decided to do another biography. But who to profile this time? He first considered Edgar Allan Poe but quickly dismissed that idea, since Poe's life was so dark. "If I wrote about him," Sid said, "I'd have to be fitted for a straitjacket." The subject he finally fastened on was an inspired one: Mark Twain, who, like Sid, was both a brilliant humorist and a natural entertainer, though Sid felt it would be "intimidating to be around a man who was 'on' all the time." Maybe so, but Sid's life of the great humorist was, reviewers agreed, "spot on."

A third biography, then? Well, why not? But, again, who should be the subject? Sid's first thought seems an unlikely one: actor John Wayne, whom Sid had come to know when he wrote the screenplay for the Duke's movie *Blood Alley*. But, on second thought, Sid abandoned this idea. "He was a sweet man," he told me, "but I couldn't stand his politics."

Nevertheless, it was the movies that ultimately provided another inspired choice: Charlie Chaplin, whose silent films, Sid explained, "had the entire world laughing without saying a word." Yet, it is the words in Sid's just published biography, *Sir Charlie*, that I predict will have the whole world laughing.

Sid was a thoroughgoing professional who always had thoughtful things to say about writing. He explained to me, for example, that he learned plotting from inventing magic tricks, which he called his "little three-act plays," each one having a beginning, a middle, and an end. This didn't mean he carefully planned plot and structure in advance. On the contrary, his strategy was to sit down at his computer every morning and say to it, "Surprise me!"

Biography offered him a different set of challenges, since his subject matter "is served up to you like oysters on a plate." Because the writer always knows where the story is going in a biography, Sid felt, "it's hard to get on a creative roll." Even so, Sid's finished work, seamless and salutary, never reflected that. Perhaps it was because the entertainer in Sid dictated that he make "theatrical decisions" in selecting scenes and incidents that would "play well" on the page that was his stage.

Sadly, Sid passed away on March 17 at the ripe old age of ninety, writing to the end. It's hard not to think that when he left the stage, he took much of the magic of children's literature with him. But what an act he gave us over the course of his long life, and most importantly, he always left us laughing!

June 1 and 15, 2010 • *Booklist*

7

THE LIVES THAT LATE THEY LED

Biography

I'VE ALWAYS BEEN a devotee of biography; I remember with special fondness the celebrated Childhood of Famous Americans series. Surely you remember the orange books with their silhouette illustrations published by Bobbs Merrill? They had titles like *George Carver, Boy Scientist*; *Clara Barton, Girl Nurse*; *Michael Cart, Boy Librarian*—okay I made that last one up, but you get the idea: kids were supposed to be inspired by reading about the childhoods of, well, famous Americans. Perhaps it was reading those books long, long ago that became the inspiration for my having grown up to write two biographies myself. You can read about one of them in the column I call "A Writer's Life." It turns out that not everybody regards biography as highly as I do, though; I give you the column called "A Disease of English Literature." Perhaps what we need as a counterweight is a series called Adulthood of Famous Americans? What do you think?

A Disease of English Literature

ACCORDING TO MY trusty *American Heritage Dictionary,* biography is "an account of a person's life written, composed or produced by another."

Well, that's simple and straightforward enough, but it's not the end of the story. Far from it. Others have defined it more, well, colorfully. Take poet and critic T. S. Eliot, for example, who asserted, "Biographies are generally a disease of English literature." Novelist Bernard Malamud didn't go quite that far, saying simply that "all biography is ultimately fiction."

On the other hand, Lytton Strachey, himself no mean biographer, more positively called it "the most delicate and humane of all the branches of the art of writing."

Yes, but does it get the job done? Apparently, the great novelist Virginia Woolf thought not, for she once wrote, "A biography is considered complete if it merely accounts for six or seven selves while a person may well have as many [as a] thousand."

Mark Twain was another naysayer. "Biographies," he observed, "are but the clothes and buttons of the man—the biography of the man himself cannot be written." I'm glad that the late Sid Fleischman didn't take that to heart; otherwise, he might not have written his delightful Twain biography, *The Trouble Begins at Eight,* or his equally diverting lives of Charlie Chaplin and Houdini.

Lest we confuse biography with other disciplines, the British novelist and humorist E. C. Bentley has helpfully noted, "The Art of Biography / Is different from Geography, / Geography is about Maps, / But Biography is about Chaps." (This is from the *Introduction to Biography for Beginners,* a collection of his famous clerihews. His what? His clerihews, brief, whimsical, four-line biographical poems; for example, "Sir Humphrey Davy / Abominated gravy. / He lived in the odium / Of having discovered sodium." The term "clerihew" itself is borrowed from Bentley's full name; that is, Edmund Clerihew Bentley.)

More seriously, one discipline with which biography is often intimately associated is history. In that regard, the essayist and philosopher Ralph Waldo Emerson once wrote the following: "We are always coming up with the emphatic facts of history in our private experience and verifying them here. All history becomes subjective; in other words, there is properly no history; only biography." Historian Thomas Carlyle said it more succinctly:

"The history of the world is but the biography of great men." For a demonstration of that, look no further than Candace Fleming's superlative *The Family Romanov,* which is not only a collective biography of the Romanovs but also an absorbing history of their time. (It's not for nothing that the book's subtitle is *Murder, Rebellion, and the Fall of Imperial Russia*.)

It is also an object lesson in one reason why we read biography: for pleasure. In my starred *Booklist* review, I called Fleming's work "fascinating, absorbing as any novel, and the stuff of an altogether memorable reading experience."

Speaking of reading experiences, I absolutely doted on biography when I was a kid, though as an adult, I realize I wasn't looking for art; I was looking for information, especially when the subject was an author. For from a very early age, I was keenly aware that books didn't write themselves; they were written by human beings about whom I was intensely curious (or was I just snoopy?). By the time I was in the fourth grade—or thereabouts—I knew I wanted to be a writer when I grew up, and I think I was curious to see if the writers I read about were like me or had been when they were kids. I also wanted to find out how they became writers. And I guess, in the midst of all this, I was looking for role models, too, another good reason for young people to read biography. I thought of that earlier this year when I reviewed a biography by Amy Houts of the TV personality Rachel Maddow (*Rachel Maddow: Primetime Political Commentator*), whose life as an out lesbian—I noted in the review—has been distinguished by a number of "firsts": she was one of only two openly gay students in her freshman class at Stanford; the first openly gay recipient of the prestigious Rhodes Scholarship; and the first openly gay person to host a prime-time news show on TV—a terrific role model, in short, for LGBTQ kids, who, historically, have had too few such in books to read.

But I digress. Back to biography and role models. In that context, I think we read biography not only to learn what we want to be but how we want to be. How do we want to conduct our lives, how do we want to comport ourselves, what qualities do we see in the books' subjects that we'd like to emulate? On the other hand, sometimes we see how we don't want to be; for example, like the Nazis, whom the young Dane Knud Pedersen and his friends in the Churchill Club bravely fought during World War II. You can read their story in Phillip Hoose's new biography, *The Boys Who Challenged Hitler.*

And lastly, we read for inspiration. Case in point: *Unbroken,* Laura Hillenbrand's life of Louis Zamperini, Olympics competitor and, later, prisoner of war, whose courage and determination helped him triumph over all odds.

So is biography, as Eliot asserted, a disease? On the contrary, it seems to me to be a sovereign remedy for the dispirited, a cure for the discouraged, and, yes, a tonic and inspiration for the rest of us. If I were a doctor, this would be my prescription: take two biographies, and call me in the morning!

June 1 and 15, 2015 • *Booklist*

So Many Lives, So Little Space

I'VE BEEN BUSY working up a sweat, once again rearranging parts of my book collections. This burst of activity has been partly for pleasure and partly for purpose. As for the former, well, if for Kenneth Grahame's Water Rat, nothing was finer than messing about with boats, for me, there is nothing more sublimely pleasant than messing about with books. As for the latter, the purpose-driven part, that is, I was trying to consolidate some collections preparatory to buying four more bookcases to put in my bedroom.

What this effort entailed was moving the contents of one seven-foot-tall bookcase from the living room into a similar one in the room I call the library. Into the library went a case of adult books—some sets (Tennyson, Dostoevsky, Arnold Bennett, etc.) and my collections of Gore Vidal, John Cheever, and Anthony Powell. Into the living room went part of my collection of British children's and young adult books. This means that virtually all of my adult and British kids' books are now in the same room(s). I say "almost," since I still have one bookcase in the living room with sets of Jane Austen, Charles Dickens, Robert Louis Stevenson, Edgar Allan Poe, Mark Twain, and Nathaniel Hawthorne that must go into the library. To make room for them, my Walter R. Brooks and L. Frank Baum collections must go upstairs to be integrated into my American children's and young adult books that are shelved there.

That's a whole lot of schlepping going on. And even then, what to do with my collections of books about books, humor, and fairy tales and folktales that are also in the library? And what will I do with the collections of Americana, graphic novels, and literary criticism and history that are upstairs? The answer—if there is an answer—is that as many of these ancillary collections as possible will be squeezed into those four new bookcases, thus freeing up desperately needed space for more young adult books, many of which—I blush to admit—are presently in boxes (the horror, the horror!).

If you're wondering what all this has to do with biography, this issue's spotlight topic, wonder no more, gentle readers, for I'm about to tell you. You see, all of this moving of books and planning where to move even more has meant a great deal of wandering around the house looking at books and discovering—serendipitously—how many of them are biographies and, to a lesser extent, autobiographies. Not a few of these are books I had forgotten I owned. This forgetting leads to occasional frustration. For example, I was in Boston several weeks ago and was thrilled to find, in a used bookstore there, a biography of L. Frank Baum (*L. Frank Baum: Creator of Oz*, by Katharine M. Rogers). Hot dog! I thought; here's a perfect companion to my Oz books. Of course, you know what happened next: I got home and discovered I already had a copy. Oh, well, into the book-donation box the second copy goes.

Not only have I forgotten I had certain books, but I haven't a clue where or when I acquired many of them. An exception may be this joint biography of the Brothers Grimm (*Paths through the Forest*, by Murray B. Peppard). It's a first edition published in 1971, but I can tell I bought it used because of the price penciled on the flyleaf ($4.50, if you must know). I'm not quite sure when I bought it, but it might have been in the mid-1980s, since there's an article laid in that I clipped from the May 1986 issue of *Smithsonian Magazine:* "From the Bookish Brothers Grimm, a Flood of Fantasy." (Time out while I read the article. OK, I'm done. Time in.) On the other hand, here's a beautiful first edition of *The Life of Sir Arthur Conan Doyle,* by the late, great mystery novelist John Dickson Carr, who specialized in locked-room mysteries. The book was published in 1949, and I also bought it used, but I have no idea when. On still another hand (that's three hands, but who's counting?), here's Jackie Wullschlager's *Hans Christian Andersen: The Life of a Storyteller,* published in 2000, and I know I bought it new.

If you're starting to get the idea that most of the biographies in my collections are of writers, you would be *keerect!* I've always had an insatiable curiosity about the lives of the people who write the books I read and collect. Some of these are harder to find than others. I have only one biography each, for example, of Robert Lawson and Robert McCloskey. Some are so hard to find that I've had to (ahem) write them myself; hence *Presenting Robert Lipsyte* and *Talking Animals and Others: The Life and Work of Walter R. Brooks, Creator of Freddy the Pig.* Still others are more—shall we say—copious. Thus, I have a clutch of lives of Lewis Carroll, Kenneth Grahame, Kate Greenaway, Randolph Caldecott, and of Dickens, Austen, Hawthorne, and so on.

For some reason, it's much easier to find biographies of children's authors than of young adult authors. In fact, aside from the Lipsyte title, I only have one life of Robert Cormier (Patty Campbell's *Robert Cormier: Daring to Disturb the Universe*) and memoirs by Jack Gantos (*Hole in My Life*) and Chris Crutcher (*King of the Mild Frontier*). Beyond these, I've got zip. Isn't it time that some enterprising publisher introduced a series of trade biographies of leading young adult authors? Of course, come to think of it, I'm sure there are excellent series from institutional publishers. Perhaps I'll do my homework and devote next year's spotlight column to them.

In the meantime forget the reading, it's back to the rearranging!

June 1 and 15, 2012 • *Booklist*

Get a Life!

ACCORDING TO THE *Oxford English Dictionary,* the first appearance in print of the somewhat sneering phrase "get a life" was in 1983 in a *Washington Post* article: "I mean, get a life!" I'm surprised it was so recent, since I would have presumed that even back in prehistoric days the phrase was being bandied about by your typical, go-getting cave dweller. As in the following (imagined) scene:

[Lights come up on solitary caveman named Ugh who is sitting watching the grass grow. Enter stage left a second caveman named Erg. He is carrying a spear.]

Erg: Hey, Ugh. What you do?

Ugh: Me watch grass grow.

Erg: Hoo-boy! You need get life. Come with me. Help kill saber-toothed tiger. There one now [pointing offstage right].

Ugh: No, thanks.

Erg: C'mon, dude! It easy. I show you. [He exits stage right.]

Erg [offstage—voice distant]: See? Now I spear saber-toothed tiger. Ei-yeeeeee!

[Voice cut short, followed by crunching and the tiger's lip-smacking sounds.]

Ugh: Better to not have life.

Why do I think Ugh was a distant ancestor of mine? Oh, yeah: because I don't have a life, either. Unless you believe sitting around all day thinking up Freddy the Pig trivia questions is a life.

Of course, even if I weren't thinking up Freddy the Pig trivia, I'd still be sitting around all day reading and writing. I mean, that's my so-called life, dudes. The best I can do is pull a biography off the nearest shelf and borrow the biographee's life vicariously, being careful, of course, to avoid bios of folks like Theodore Roosevelt, that inveterate advocate of "the strenuous life."

"I preach to you, then, my countrymen," he told the members of the Hamilton Club of Chicago, "that our country calls not for the life of ease but for the life of strenuous endeavor."

To quote the immortal words of Ugh, "Better to not have life."

Okay, all kidding aside, I have always enjoyed reading biographies, even those of TR, who—when he wasn't busy galloping on horseback up San

Juan Hill—was passionately reading books and writing them. And, heaven knows, my favorite biographies are literary ones. The trouble is, there aren't enough of them, especially for young readers. But it's not because writers don't have lives; they do! It's just that (1) those lives aren't much valued in these United States of Benightedness, and (2) kids who don't like to read in the first place are not about to cozy up to a pile of biographies of the guys (and gals) who write same.

To find out just how few literary biographies are published for young readers, I turned to last year's Spotlight on Biography issue and discovered that of the twenty-five titles reviewed in the Books for Youth section, only one—Jane Yolen's *Lost Boy,* a picture-book biography of Sir James M. Barrie—was of the literary persuasion. And that's not an anomaly. Since 2003, a mere 10 have been reviewed, 4 of them being of 2 writers: Mark Twain and Zora Neale Hurston and a single title each about Louisa May Alcott, James M. Barrie, L. Frank Baum, Ernest Hemingway, Mary Shelley, and Henry David Thoreau.

I haven't seen all of these, unfortunately, but I do have the Baum biography; it's by Kathleen Krull, who has also given us a wonderful biography of Dr. Seuss and the droll collective biography *Lives of the Writers: Comedies, Tragedies, and What the Neighbors Thought.*

Another Baum biography is coauthored by the late Jean Shirley and her daughter, Angelica Shirley Carpenter. On her own, Angelica has also written biographies of Robert Louis Stevenson, Frances Hodgson Burnett, and Lewis Carroll.

There is no shortage of adult biographies of Baum, who actually had a life that included experiences ranging from raising chickens (!) to plying the Broadway stage. But our interest here is books published for young readers, and in that context, the one author of those listed above who seems to have attracted the most authorial attention is Mark Twain.

Twain had such a long (for his day) and event-filled life that most biographers tend to focus on only one or two aspects of it. Thus, in his biography *The Trouble Begins at 8,* Sid Fleischman deals only with Twain's early life and his experiences in the West. Cheryl Harness's picture-book biography *Mark Twain and the Queens of the Mississippi* focuses on the author's connections with the Mississippi River and steamboat piloting.

The newest biography, another picture book, is *The Adventures of Mark Twain by Huckleberry Finn.* It's actually by Robert Burleigh, but the conceit is that it's written by Twain's greatest creation, the incorrigible Huck. And this one does cover major events from throughout Twain's whole life. The story is helped along by Barry Blitt's terrific pen-and-ink and watercolor illustrations. I gotta tell ya, folks, I'm crazy about this book! For one thing, I love the voice Burleigh has created for Huck. An example (Huck is explaining why he's writing about Twain):

"Didn't we float down the same river, layin' by and lookin' up at the sky all speckled with stars? Didn't we climb the same hills (tolerable long and steep they was, too), and didn't we play cops and robbers in the same woods?"

This is not only a wonderful use of vernacular, it's downright poetic.

Equally wonderful are Blitt's droll pictures. Like Huck (and Twain's) tendency to tell the occasional stretcher, Blitt uses exaggeration for comedic effect, especially playing with proportion to increase or diminish the size of characters as seems appropriate. The typography also employs this technique, which suggests a spoken voice such as the one Twain used for his lectures.

Indeed, here's a book that begs to be read aloud. Too bad Twain isn't around to do it himself. But I'll do it in a pinch, for I've got lots of time, not having a life, don't you know.

June 1 and 15, 2011 • *Booklist*

Limning Lives

A CASE MIGHT be made, I suppose, that biography as a genre for young readers began with Mason Locke ("Parson") Weems, whose hagiographical life of George Washington was published for readers of all ages way back in 1800 but quickly became a staple fixture of the child's own bookshelf. If so, biography's debut was an artistically shaky but commercially successful one—like so many books that have been published for kids ever since! Weems articulated his plans for his work in a letter to his publisher, Mathew Carey: "My plan! I give his history, sufficiently minute . . . I then show that his unparrelled [*sic*] rise and elevation were owing to his Great Virtues. We can sell it with great rapidity for 25 or 37 cents, and it would not cost 10" (quoted in Leonard Marcus's *Minders of Make-Believe*).

Offering the lives of great men—and, later, women—as examples of moral rectitude and the successes that would surely follow (for both the reader and the publisher) became a staple strategy of children's publishing. Firmly rooted in the didactic, the biographies that resulted became the special province of institutional publishers, who targeted their product at the classroom, where such books were read not for pleasure but for inspiration and edification, moral and otherwise.

No wonder, then, that, as Mary Mehlman Burns wrote in *Children's Books and Their Creators,* "until the mid-nineteen seventies, biography was the stepchild among the genres of children's literature." Ah, but then, at last, along came the laudable likes of Jean Fritz and Russell Freedman, and suddenly, biography became not only literarily respectable but also a joy to read. Partly this was due to the expository talents Fritz and Freedman brought to their texts. Partly it was due to the increasingly attractive design and visual content of the biographies that burgeoned in the wake of Freedman's 1987 *Lincoln: A Photobiography,* which, copping a Newbery Medal, brought new critical and popular attention to the genre.

And partly it was a function of a number of other trends that began changing publishing for young readers in the 1980s and thereafter. The rise of the picture book in the 1980s, for example, brought readers distinguished picture-book biographies by Diane Stanley, Aliki, Kathleen Krull, and others. The rise of narrative nonfiction for adults, coupled with both the revolution in the design and illustration of books for young readers pioneered by Dorling Kindersley in its Eyewitness books, and also the attendant shift of the market from institutional to trade, brought irresistibly readable and gorgeously illustrated books such as Elizabeth Partridge's Printz Honor-winning *John Lennon: All I Want Is the Truth* and her earlier *This Land Was Made for You and Me: The Life and Times of Woody Guthrie.* Other noteworthy examples include George Sullivan's *Berenice Abbot, Photographer;* Sid Fleischman's *Escape! The Story of the Great Houdini;* Jan Greenberg and Sandra Jordan's *Runaway Girl: The Artist, Louise Bourgeois;* and James Cross Giblin's Sibert Award-winning *The Life and Death of Adolf Hitler.* Evidence of the new literary stature of biography is the fact that since the inception of the Sibert Award (for "informational" books) in 2001, fully half of the Sibert Medals have been awarded to biography. In addition to *Hitler,* these include Marc Aronson's *Sir Walter Ralegh and the Quest for El Dorado,* Russell Freedman's *The Voice That Changed a Nation: Marian Anderson and the Struggle for Equal Rights,* and Peter Sís's picture book for all ages *The Wall: Growing Up behind the Iron Curtain,* a book in which virtually all of these trends converge.

Two other trends have added both interest and artistic weight to the field of biography. Interestingly, both began as trends in the publishing of fiction. First is the rise of the graphic novel, which has now resulted in such graphic nonfiction works as Judd Winick's *Pedro and Me* (a Sibert Honor Book), James Sturm and Rich Tommaso's *Satchel Paige: Striking Out Jim Crow,* and the Malaysian cartoonist Lat's two absolutely irresistible autobiographies, *Kampung Boy* and *Town Boy.* A second trend grows out of the rise of the novel in verse and has recently given us such biographies in verse as Marilyn Nelson's two luminous works, *Carver: A Life in Poems* and *A Wreath for Emmett Till,* and Stephanie Hemphill's Printz Honor winner *Your Own Sylvia: A Verse Portrait of Sylvia Plath.*

Perhaps the most recent trend in the field of limning lives is another that has "trickled down" from adult publishing: the memoir of (often dysfunctional) childhood and adolescence, pioneered by Tobias Wolff's *This Boy's Life,* which is also an early example of the currently popular crossover book with appeal to both adults and young adults. Then there is Jack Gantos's *A Hole in My Life,* an example of a memoir published as a young adult book. And most recently we have Nic Sheff's *Tweak: Growing Up on Methamphetamines,* which has garnered great media attention thanks to the fact that the author's father, David Sheff, has written his own memoir of his son's battle with addiction; titled *Beautiful Boy,* it was published as an adult title, though both books have quintessential crossover appeal. And speaking of crossover: yes, the line between memoir and novel seems to be increasingly blurry, thanks in part to such adult books as James Frey's *A Million Little Pieces* and Augusten Burroughs's seemingly endless supply of his own memoirs. If this aspect trickles down to books for young readers, we may find ourselves coming full circle, back to Parson Weems, who, let us not forget, created, out of the whole cloth of his imagination, the story of Washington, his little hatchet, and that legendary cherry tree. Plus ca change . . .

June 1 and 15, 2008 • *Booklist*

A Writer's Life

TWENTY OR SO years ago I took a leave of absence from my then day job as director of the Beverly Hills Public Library to start work on a biography of my hero, the children's book author Walter R. Brooks. I actually managed to write about 100 pages of the book before I had to return to work as librarian to the stars and relegate the project to the proverbial back burner. And there it stayed, along with countless other of my good intentions (mine is a *big* back burner), until about six months ago when a small publishing house in San Diego, Hungry Tiger Press (which specializes in the work of another American children's book writer, L. Frank Baum), offered to publish the book. That was the good news. The bad news? Now I have to actually finish writing the infernal thing.

I've already taken the first step: I've reread what I wrote those two decades ago and, with a wince and a deep sigh, thrown most of it away. Oh, I kept the first sentence ("It snowed—and then some—in Rome, New York, the morning Walter R. Brooks was born") and a few others, too, but I quickly realized that much of the rest was more of a love letter to my research than to the life I was trying to limn.

I suppose that's a problem that any biographer faces. One spends years, after all, poking about in records, uncovering a stray fact here, an insight there, raising new questions that can only be answered by visiting all the places the author once called "home," talking—if you're lucky—with people who knew your subject (mine died fifty years ago), and realizing, after a while, that trying to reconstruct a human life really is like trying to put together a jigsaw puzzle containing thousands of pieces, most of which are missing. So surely you can be forgiven for trying to make use of every one of the hard-won facts you've managed to piece together. But as a result, after writing those 100 pages, I had progressed no further than the year 1901 when Walter reached the grand old age of fifteen! Ooops. This is not because I was painting such a lovingly detailed portrait of his, uh, early years. On the contrary, much of the stuff I had written wasn't even about him but, rather, about his ancestors, who, truth to tell, led more eventful lives than he did.

Of course, that's why writing a literary biography is, to put it mildly, such a challenge. How many ways are there of saying, "And then he wrote?" For Walter was one of those writers who spent his days quietly . . . writing.

Ah, but his ancestors—that's a different story! His paternal grandfather, Squire Stevens, followed the 1849 gold rush from Rome, New York, to California, as did two of his sons (Walter's uncles); a third went to sea at the age of twelve; another was killed by Apache Indians in Arizona. Hot dog! And then, even better, having made his fortune in California, Grandpa Stevens returned to Rome and was elected mayor, became president of two banks, and started the Rome Iron Works. He was, in the great American tradition, a mover, a shaker, and a capitalist par excellence.

As for Walter's paternal grandfather and namesake, Dr. Walter R. Brooks was a distinguished theologian and an amateur naturalist who, in the 1870s, taught natural history at Madison University (which today is Colgate). He was also pastor of the local Baptist church, and he struggled to harmonize the teachings of the church with the writings of Charles Darwin, whom he admired. Dr. B. was not only an intellectual, you see, but also a deeply original thinker whose work, one associate wrote, "revolutionized the thinking of the place" (Madison, that is). He also had the good sense to marry an heiress, and he and his new wife became leaders of high society as it was then lived in Hamilton, New York.

I don't know why I find this stuff so fascinating—but I do, actually. One reason, of course, is that it brings me closer to Walter, whom, alas, I never met; a second and more important reason is that all of this ancestral stuff conspired to shape the man and the writer that Walter would become. Like Dr. Brooks, he loved the natural world; during the summers he spent in his cabin in the Catskills, his favorite pastime was helping out on the neighboring farm; no wonder, then, that he wrote so brilliantly—and affectionately—about pigs and cows and ducks and cats and horses and goats. But he also wrote, less affectionately and with a deftly satirical pen, about human animals—politicians and rich folks, especially bankers. And like his namesake grandfather, Walter, too, "rejected sham and artificiality." And maybe that's why he named his pet cocker spaniel, an unusually greedy dog, "Squire."

In the twenty years since I back-burnered my original manuscript, I've learned a great deal more about my subject, but the fact is that much of what I've come to know about Walter R. Brooks derives from a close reading of his work, published and unpublished. Though I suspect Walter would have denied it, he does seem to have put an awful lot of himself into his books. As for the man who is emerging from those words—well, back in the days when I used to interview authors for my cable TV show *In Print*, a favorite question for biographers was, "Did your feelings about your subject change as you were writing his/her biography?"

My own answer? Heck, no. I liked the guy when I started the project, and I like him, if anything, even more now. For, after all, who could dislike the man who created Freddy the Pig? And who, in virtually every word he ever wrote, celebrated the enduring importance of friendship.

June 1 and 15, 2007 • *Booklist*

8

TRIBUTES

Memories and Memorials

IT'S NOT BY accident that this is the longest chapter in the book. It's by design and is rooted in my firm belief that, as Arthur Miller put it in *Death of a Salesman*, "Attention must be paid." I'm distressed by how few people I encounter these days know names like Charlotte Zolotow, Zena Sutherland, Bill Morris, Myra Cohn Livingston, and on and on. These people were giants and their contributions to literature were gigantic. We need to remember them and so I have tried, in my small way, to memorialize them in my columns. You'll find that I have memorialized buildings, too: the libraries that have informed and enriched my life. Consider this chapter, then, an extended exercise in celebration of people, places, and books that are especially dear to my heart. Which is why you'll find two columns here about Walter R. Brooks and his famous Freddy the Pig books, for Freddy is, of course, the pig o' my heart. And you'll find that I conclude this book with a nod to the man who started it: one of my heroes, America's former Poet Laureate, Donald Hall.

My Churches

I GREW UP in Logansport, Indiana, a small town located in a valley at the confluence of two rivers: the Eel and the more famous Wabash (Paul Dresser's "On the Banks of the Wabash Far Away" is Indiana's state song). Thanks to the rivers, Logansport came to be known as "the City of Bridges." But it's also, less officially, the city of churches. Growing up, I seemed to find one on every corner. My own church, St. James Lutheran, for example, stood at the corner of Ninth and Spear Streets, across the street from the Ninth Street Christian Church (which my grandmother attended) and a block away from St. Vincent de Paul Catholic Church. On the keystone above the entrance to my church were incised the words *Sankt Jakobi Evangelische Luthereinische Kirche*, which acknowledged its nineteenth-century German immigrant founders. Every Sunday you could find me and my twin sister at St. James, taken there (often kicking and screaming!) for Sunday school and church. So often were we there—not only for church but for vacation Bible school (some vacation!) and, later, for confirmation classes—it's no wonder that at one time I could recite all the books of the Bible by heart (Genesis, Exodus, Leviticus, Numbers, Deuteronomy and so on and so forth). I could also name the 12 apostles and recite the 10 Commandments and the Apostles' Creed. Heck, I even knew the story of Balaam and his donkey. But that's a tale for another time.

To get back to churches: don't tell my mother, but St. James wasn't my only one. I had a second. It didn't stand on a corner, though. It stood halfway between Sixth and Seventh Streets on Broadway, across the street and down the block from City Hall. There was no keystone above its entrance, but there were words carved there in Indiana limestone. They were *Free to All*. Yes, my second church was the Logansport–Cass County Public Library, and that's where you might find me worshipping secular books and reading on any day but Sunday. My favorite time to be at the library was Friday evening, when—aside from a token staffer—I might be the only one in the reading room. It gave me a proprietary feeling, as if some day all of what I saw would be mine. Of course, it was when, years later, I became that library's director. I also became secretary of my church congregation, but let me not get ahead of myself.

If I was a member of St. James, I was also a member of the library; my library card proved it. I got my first card when I was seven years old; its number was 12927 (half the time I can't remember my own phone number, but I've never forgotten my library card number). If St. James ministered to my soul, the library ministered to my mind. Together, I'd like to think they civilized me. And if the Reverend Alfred C. Gerni was my pastor, Mary Annetta Holmes, city librarian for fully fifty years, was my mentor.

Growing up with the knowledge that I would need to find a part-time job as soon as I could get a worker's permit, I dreamed of working at only one place; some dreamed of employment at the Sycamore Drive-In, some at the local Dairy Queen, but me? I dreamed of the library. How was I to realize the dream, though? Well, church played a part in that, too. I've already told you that my grandmother was a member of the Ninth Street Christian Church; so, as fate would have it, was Miss Holmes. And all it took was a word in her ear from my grandmother one Sunday to make me the newest employee of the library. I began my proud service there as a page, shelving books, reading shelves, retrieving magazines for patrons (the magazine stacks were in the basement), emptying the book bin, and so on. My favorite of these jobs was shelf reading in the juvenile stacks. Because the library's collections had never been weeded (I'm not kidding), examining each volume on the shelves to ensure it was in the right place was a kind of de facto education in the history of children's literature. No wonder I fell in love with the genre. It was all humble work to be sure, but if I were the best little boy in the world (and I was!), I was also determined to be the best little employee in the world (and I was!!). And so I advanced through the ranks, helping with the summer reading program, answering phones, and—welcome to the big time—working at the circulation desk, where I had regular contact with the library's patrons. That was sometimes a mixed blessing, but it certainly widened my circle of acquaintances. I venture to say I knew more senior citizens than any other kid in town.

In my own senior years, I find myself often thinking about the library and about St. James and their areas of commonality. One I haven't mentioned is their blessed quiet. If you have ever read a Little Golden Book called *Noises and Mr. Flibberty Jib,* you'll know that, even as a young teenager, I was Mr. Flibberty Jib. For me, silence was truly golden. No, I didn't bustle about the library shushing people, and the place wasn't always sepulchrally quiet, but there was a generally peaceful air about it, as there was about church. It was an invitation to relax and think, and I had found a sanctuary in both; they were places where the worst of the world was held at bay and where you could simply be yourself and feel, yes, that this was a place where you belonged. A tonic for a sometimes troubled teenager and, still today, a kind of *sanctum sanctorum* for the senior adult I've become.

Thanks for both.

November 15, 2013 • *Booklist*

A Clean, Well Lighted Sanctuary

NOW THAT NATIONAL LIBRARY WEEK 2000 and its imperative, grab-you-by-the-lapels and shout-in-your-face theme "Read! Learn! Connect! @ the Library" are just memories, I find myself wondering how you observed this annual occasion—aside from reading *Booklist*, that is. Perhaps you kicked things off on Saturday, April 8, by joining in the observation of "Connect for Kids" day. Cosponsored by the ALA and the Benton Foundation, this was a nationwide event—no, make that an opportunity—to highlight the variety of resources available at community libraries for America's kids and their families.

Or maybe you joined the National Endowment for the Arts, the Center for the Book in the Library of Congress, and other organizations in sponsoring Live at the Library 2000 and launching a yearlong celebration of the arts.

Or, speaking of the arts, maybe you followed the Children's Book Council's lead and observed Young People's Poetry Week (April 10–16), an event established in 1999 as part of National Poetry Month. If you're not familiar with the Children's Book Council and its many other excellent programs, check out its website (www.cbcbooks.org). Tell 'em Carte Blanche sent you.

As for me? Well, I celebrated the usual way by taking yet another trip down that well-worn thoroughfare, Memory Lane, where I forged some more links in my chain of memories about the libraries in my life.

I started connecting with libraries when, at the age of seven, I got my first library card. At that time the Logansport Public Library used Gaylord charging machines to circulate materials, and that meant my card came equipped with a metal plate on which was embossed my number, which I immediately memorized and have never forgotten. It was 12927. When you checked out a book, the clerk would insert your card in one slot of the charging machine, and the book card in a second. There was a wonderfully satisfying punching sound, and—hey, presto!—the card number was printed on the book card. This meant that you (and the rest of the world if it were interested) could then see, by looking at the card in the book pocket, whether or not you had borrowed that title or, if you had, how many times. Inveterate rereader that I was, it was not uncommon to see 12927 appear upwards of a dozen times on cards in the Freddy the Pig book pockets, or those in copies of the Oz books and the Thornton W. Burgess animal stories.

Twenty years later, by the way, when I became director of the library, I got a new library card with a new number: 1. I had arrived!

Because the public library provided deposit collections, each elementary school in Logansport had a library. The second link in my library chain was forged at one of those; it was located on the second floor at McKinley School between the first- and fourth-grade classrooms. We kids were taken to the library once a week where we were permitted to choose one or two books, and I still remember my immense satisfaction at beating my friend Jeanie Yoder to the shelf that housed a book we both coveted: it was called *School Days in Disneyville*, and it featured stories about the Disney characters as students in grade school.

My first library "job" came several years later when I was in fourth grade at Columbia Elementary School, and my teacher, Miss Beatty, selected me to be a library helper. The other guys wanted to be patrol boys. Not me—I wanted to be a librarian! This may tell you more about me as a ten-year-old than I care to reveal, but it's too late now.

My first paying job came at the end of my freshman year in high school when I was hired as a page at the public library. I guess the librarian, Miss Holmes, decided she might as well put me on the payroll because I was there practically every day anyway. I continued to work at the library every summer until I graduated from college in 1963.

During the academic year at Northwestern University, where I earned my undergraduate degree, I worked twenty hours per week as an assistant in the rare book room at the Charles Deering Library, a vaguely medieval-looking monstrosity that, according to campus legend, had been described by Frank Lloyd Wright as resembling "a pregnant pig on its back."

I didn't much care what the building looked like, though. I treasured it for its contents. It was my first introduction to the wealth of resources I could connect with in the stacks of a university library. I could get lost in those windowless stacks, but who cared, because each new range revealed another serendipitous discovery. I'll never forget the day I discovered a complete run of the *Baker Street Journal*, the official publication of the Baker Street Irregulars, the celebrated Sherlock Holmes fan club. I wasn't an Irregular, but I was a big Sherlock Holmes fan. I also discovered back files of the *New Yorker* and spent hours—when I should have been studying—poring over old issues and reading profiles by Wolcott Gibbs, drama reviews by Robert Benchley, and those celebrated "Newsbreaks" that filled space at the end of columns.

When I wasn't in the stacks or working in the rare book room, where my principal job seemed to be watering the sponges that provided a rudimentary kind of climate control in the glass-covered bookcases, I was lounging in the browsing room, which offered not only a marvelously eclectic collection of books but also the most comfortable leather chairs I've ever sunk into. It was there, one luxuriously lazy afternoon, that I read in a single sitting *Alice in Wonderland,* a book I had struggled to read as a kid but to no avail. For me, the right time to read *Alice* turned out to be that undergraduate afternoon in the Deering Library.

My next library was Columbia University's Butler Library, which housed the graduate library school. My favorite place in that building was the main reference room with its two-tiered reference stacks. I loved climbing to the second level, which was filled with alcoves created by the configuration of the stacks. In each alcove was a single study carrel located next to a window. You could sit at the carrel and read for hours, glancing, from time to time, either out the window on one side or over the railing on the other side, admiring their respective views of exterior and interior worlds.

Remembering this place invokes the same feelings that my memories of all of these libraries do. It's the feeling that, I'll bet, Ernest Hemingway experienced when he wrote the resonant phrase "a clean, well lighted place," a place that banishes darkness and its demons, a place that is unfailingly snug and secure, a place that is . . . well, sanctuary.

That's why I love libraries and my memories of them—because they connect me with books and reading and learning, yes, but also because they unfailingly offer me a clean, well-lighted sanctuary when the world outside becomes too much to bear.

Perhaps the theme of next year's National Library Week could be "Read! Learn! Connect! And Find Sanctuary! @ the Library."

It has a nice ring, doesn't it?

April 15, 2000 • *Booklist*

Among the Digitally Divided

THIS MORNING WHILE I was gasping and wheezing my way through my daily three-mile run, I found my thoughts straying, for some reason, to statements that may have sounded reasonable when first spoken but that in retrospect seem to invite—no, demand—reconsideration. Statements like, "Michael, you'll love running, and it's so good for you." Or, "You know, Michael, a barking dog never bites." Or, "Don't be silly, Michael, you're not having a heart attack, that's just indigestion."

Such statements are nothing new, of course; they've been around since the dawn of time, the classic example being, "Oh, for heaven's sake, Adam. It's just an apple. Take a bite."

Mind you, that last one may be a paraphrase, since I wasn't around to hear Eve say it, but, nevertheless, in its global impact, I rank it right up there with the statement I actually have been hearing uttered—or sputtered—a lot lately, usually by school board or city council members at budget review time. Maybe you've heard it, too. It goes something like this: "Why, shoot! We don't need libraries anymore. Kids have computers and the Internet now."

Why, shoot! You and I know what crazy talk that is, for too many reasons to articulate here. But, for starters, someone surely needs to point out to these keepers of the keys and purse strings that not every kid does have a computer and an Internet connection. Nor does every adult, including—at the present moment—me. Family business has brought me back to my hometown of Logansport, Indiana, and a two-week stay at my ninety-year-old mother's house, which is equipped with what I presume to be the last rotary-dial phone left in America. As a result, I can't use the laptop that I never leave home without to access the online environment; heck, I can't even call the message center back in sunny San Diego to access my voice mail or, for that matter, to use any other form of automated phone service that requires a telephone keypad. To do that, I have to walk to the neighborhood drugstore to use the pay phone there. As for computer access, I have to go to—you guessed it—the local public library, the only source of public-access computers in all of Cass County, Indiana. (Internet cafes are apparently regarded as the devil's playground hereabouts, and the local City Council yesterday voted down a proposal to pursue a community-wide wireless Internet access program.)

Not surprisingly, then, an extraordinary number of other people—have-nots of every age—line up alongside me every day to use one of the three available machines at the library (there would be a fourth but it crashed the day it was installed, the staff tell me, and has yet to be repaired or replaced). This is my first personal experience of being on the wrong side of the famous digital divide and, frankly, it stinks! Or to put it less inelegantly, it's deeply disquieting to see firsthand the ever-expanding breadth of the divide and to be reminded that having limited or, worse, no electronic access to the wealth of information available online is, in many ways, to be made a nonperson, or at least an intellectually impoverished person.

But, of course, that's only part of the problem. Consider that when, after waiting in a queue for an hour or more, I finally manage to get my hands on one of the precious public computers, I find that roughly half the time I can't access the Internet, a too-common problem, I'm told, with the local server. Well, golleee, as Gomer Pyle used to say, what next?

Something a lot worse, I suspect, than Cart being unable to get his e-mail or read the *Washington Post* online. I had a taste of this "something worse" a month or so ago when, flying home from a trip to St. Petersburg, Russia (great art, wonderful architecture, lousy coffee), I arrived at the San Francisco International Airport to find U.S. Customs in a state of rampant chaos, literally not figuratively. Why? Because the airport's computer system had crashed. And, without the computer, no one even remotely official knew what to do—except to run around wringing their hands.

Vastly worse, of course, was the nightmare scenario created by Hurricane Katrina when not only computers but civilization itself seemed to crash. The one good thing to come out of that unspeakable natural disaster was its imperative demand that we confront the heartbreaking extent of poverty in the richest nation on earth, the second-class citizenship that seems to be the best we can offer to the poor and disadvantaged, and the chasm—not the mere divide—that separates America's haves from her have-nots.

Which brings me back to the library, the one public institution which can bridge that chasm, since in the wards, precincts, and parishes of the library, there are no haves and have-nots. The library's wealth of resources, which mercifully includes not only online access but also invaluable collections of print materials (nearly 300,000 in this small-town library alone), is equally available to every member of the community. And even to drop-in visitors from halfway across the country. In fact, as I write this column, I'm sitting in the main reading room of the Logansport Public Library, a brisk ten-minute walk from my mother's house. I'll always have a soft spot in my heart for this library in which I spent such a large part of my childhood and which I grew up to direct. It's changed a lot during the thirty-two years I've been gone, of course, but one thing remains the same. Above its Indiana limestone entrance are carved three words whose simple eloquence offers the perfect rebuttal to the bland assertion that in the age of the Internet we don't need libraries any longer. What are the words? Well, I've shared them with you before in this column, but they are so fundamental to every library's mission and of such enduring importance to our civilization that they can't be repeated too often. So what are they?

Free to All, of course.

Even to those of little faith in the library's eternal indispensability!

October 15, 2005 • *Booklist*

A Love Letter to Weetzie

ONE OF THE secret pleasures of writing endlessly about books is seeing yourself quoted. There's something reassuring, even validating, about having your words invoked—especially if you're a nervous type like myself. I had this happy experience recently when my copy of the new tenth anniversary edition of Francesca Lia Block's classic-in-the-making *Weetzie Bat* arrived (yes, believe it or not, it was first published a decade ago!). As I was admiring the newly designed dust jacket with its hot pastel and neon colors, I noticed some familiar words on the verso. Though they were attributed to a corporate author, the *Los Angeles Times Book Review,* I recognized them as my own. Here they are: "One of the most original books of the last ten years."

That proud declaration first appeared in my 1991 review of Block's second novel, *Witch Baby.* Here it is in context: "The reviewer's best friend is the easy comparison: 'Leon Garfield is a 20th-century Charles Dickens. Charles Dickens is a 19th-century Leon Garfield.' And so on. Imagine the reviewer's discomfort, then, when Francesca Lia Block's first young adult novel, *Weetzie Bat,* was published, and readers discovered one of the most original books of the last 10 years. The best we critics could do was to describe it as a punk fairy tale."

Writing endlessly about books means reading them endlessly, too. And the more you read, the more you realize how derivative too much of our fiction is. That's why it's time to pop champagne corks in celebration when you discover a book that is sui generis and breathtaking in its originality—a book like *Weetzie Bat.* Oh, sure, Block's first novel showed some of its influences: Latin American magic realism, an easy familiarity with European fairy tales, a more than nodding acquaintance with Imagist poetry (I later learned that she had written her thesis on HD and Emily Dickinson), and a passion for contemporary music, punk fashion, and club culture. But thanks to the author's amazingly creative imagination, all of these elements were brought together in ways that were breathtakingly and authentically original.

When I first read *Weetzie Bat* a decade ago, I thought of it as being a fragile thing like butterfly wings. Now that it has been tamed by time, however, I realize how sturdy it is, both as a work of art and as an open-minded, nonjudgmental, sweet-spirited, generously compassionate celebration of love in all of its myriad forms and manifestations. It is love that is the heart and soul of this novel, and that is what makes it a universal work of fiction and puts the lie to the claim of some that it is a regional work. Nonsense. It's only regional if the experience of falling in love is regional.

Of course, one of its evergreen charms *is* its richly realized southern California setting. Block grew up in Studio City, California, in the shadow of Laurel Canyon. "I love the idea," she once told me, "that through this great city run little paths of nature with coyotes and deer and with wonderful ghostly memories and legends." The magician Harry Houdini lived in the Canyon, she points out, and readers of her non-Weetzie novel, *The Hanged Man*, may recognize that the ruins of Houdini's mansion provide the haunting backdrop for one of its most powerful scenes. How appropriate—and even magical—it is that she should, thus, have found real-life inspiration for Weetzie in this special setting. Here's how she described the experience in the *Los Angeles Times:* "When I was 17 years old, my friends and I used to drive through Laurel Canyon in a shiny blue vintage Mustang convertible. On one of these trips, a punk princess with spiky bleached hair, a very pink '50s prom dress and cowboy boots seemed to appear out of nowhere, her thumb up in the air. We didn't pick her up. But her image stayed in my mind: the pixie spirit of Laurel Canyon, Los Angeles." It would be several more years before the pixie got a name: "A friend and I were rocking to KROQ," Block recalls, "when we saw a pink Pinto with the license plate 'WEETZIE.' As soon as I had the name, the character just evolved by herself."

If Block was lucky in the setting of her childhood, she was even luckier in her parents. Her mother, Gilda, is a poet; her late father, Irving Alexander Block (to whom *Weetzie Bat* is dedicated), was an artist. To look at his paintings, especially his gorgeous still lifes, is to understand another source of inspiration for Weetzie and the books that followed it—all of which display a painterly appreciation for landscape and for the objects that fill individuals' lives.

Block's parents encouraged her early interest in writing. "I remember writing poems on big lined paper and being praised for that," she tells me. "I felt encouraged and wanted to keep on doing that." And so she did: her first book, *Moon Harvest*, published when she was only sixteen, is a collection of her poetry.

It's not too wide of the mark to say that another kind of magic also influenced her: movie magic. On the very first page of *Weetzie*, for example, Marilyn Monroe's hand and footprints at Grauman's (Chinese Theater) are mentioned, and two pages later, Weetzie and Dirk go to a Jayne Mansfield film festival. Mansfield, of course, will assume a mythic largeness in the character of Vixanne Wigg, Witch Baby's mother. Anyone who grows up in Los Angeles absorbs a generic Hollywood atmosphere almost by osmosis, but in Block's case, the influence was, again, more personal: before beginning his career as a fine artist, her father worked in the movies as an art director and designer of special effects, including those for the classic science fiction movie *Forbidden Planet,* which means Francesca grew up with Robbie the Robot as her "brother."

Weetzie Bat would be followed by four more novels about the eponymous heroine and her extended, nontraditional family of filmmakers and musicians. An omnibus volume, *Dangerous Angels,* was published last year, and for Block, this act brought a feeling of closure that may mean, she tells me, that there will be no more novels about the punk pixie of Laurel Canyon.

Whether or not that is so, the *Weetzie* books have a permanent place in young adult literature, and their importance in terms of freshness of vision, imaginative use of language, richness of setting, and unforgettable characters cannot be overestimated. But don't forget that underneath the fantasy is a gritty realism that fearlessly tackles cutting-edge issues such as anorexia, child abuse, AIDS, drug use, homophobia, and more. What redeems these at-risk aspects is love magic.

"Magic and love," Block says in summary, "that's the equation. I've seen it in my own life and I believe that out of love there emerge transformation and transcendence. Every time I write about this equation, I discover new expressions of it."

And so do her readers, and that, folks, is why I too LOVE *Weetzie Bat!* Its magic remains as good for my heart today as it was ten years ago. And you may quote me on that.

May 15, 1999 • *Booklist*

Descent into Limbo

IT WAS THE morning of Saturday, April 5, and the city of Cambridge, Massachusetts, was awash with anticipation, for later that day Maurice Sendak would present the 2003 May Hill Arbuthnot Honor Lecture in MIT's Kresge Auditorium. Not even the weather—rain turning to sleet turning to ice turning to snow—could, well . . . dampen the palpable sense of excitement. In fact, declared Barbara Harrison, codirector of Children's Literature New England (CLNE), "Nothing has caused such a stir in Cambridge since Paul Revere!" And you know what? Allowing for a degree of proprietary hyperbole (CLNE was cosponsor of the lecture), this visitor, for one, sensed she was right.

The wild rumpus began at 9 a.m. with a three-hour Sendak Symposium that, like virtually every other event associated with the lecture, was oversubscribed. People, it seemed, had come from every corner of the United States and even from England for the events. Happily, I was among the 250 who were privileged to attend the morning symposium and the more than 1,000 who would make up the afternoon audience for the lecture itself. (Full-disclosure moment: I was present as a member of the 2003 Arbuthnot Committee, which had selected Sendak and Cambridge as the lecturer and site, respectively. Other committee members were Joanna Rudge Long, chair; Karen Breen; Barbara Immroth; and the late Jan Smuda.) Following Barbara Harrison's welcoming remarks, her CLNE codirector, the author Gregory Maguire, jump-started the program with his "Sendak Appreciation," a lively, affectionate lecture that was, withal, one of the most extraordinary marriages of wit and erudition that I've ever heard. Noting that "we come not to bury Sendak but to praise him," Maguire went on to remind us that until Sendak, "the peril and promise of existence" had been absent from the American picture book. *Where the Wild Things Are*, the first of many Sendakian masterpieces, changed that, of course, and has remained emblematic of the author-artist's "trust in the validity of the emotions of children."

Using slides, Maguire also offered witty proof that Sendak's books are filled with "visual quotations" from the work of an "extensive and eclectic company" of other artists ranging from William Blake to Wilhelm Busch, and from William Nicholson to Winsor McCay to Beatrix Potter, whose very own walking stick Sendak carried, talisman-like, throughout the day.

Next came a panel, moderated by author Betty Levin, that examined other aspects of the Sendak career. Literary historian Leonard Marcus began by tracing the influence of Randolph Caldecott's pioneering picture books on Sendak. Michael DiCapua, Sendak's longtime editor, reminisced about their forty years of collaborative association that began with *The Bat Poet* and continues with a work-in-progress, *Brundibar,* which, with text by playwright Tony Kushner, is a retelling of a children's opera that is inextricably linked with the Holocaust. Calling it "the most demanding book Sendak has ever illustrated," DiCapua predicted it would be one of the two books for which the artist will be best remembered (along with *Wild Things,* of course).

The morning concluded with thoughts from Daryl Mark of the Cambridge Public Library on children reading Sendak. What she had to say about kids' reactions to the work at hand offered, for me, some of the morning's most compelling reasons for its enduring success, all of them rooted in one man's genius for understanding the emotional life of children and his nearly unrivaled ability to climb into the child's mind and to draw, with fidelity and respect, what he sees there.

So, that was the morning. The main event began at 1:30 that afternoon with music. How could it not? Sendak himself had acknowledged during earlier brief remarks that his "first passion" has always been music, without which he cannot "live or work." And so, to help him with the work of lecturing, the Esplanade String Quartet offered selections from a single composer, the one who, Sendak said, "has been my savior": Wolfgang Amadeus Mozart.

Following the musical greetings, equally graceful verbal ones came from local and national dignitaries. And then it was time for Joanna Long to introduce the 2003 lecturer to a packed house that welcomed him with an ovation so thunderous that it seemed, genuinely, to touch Sendak's heart. It was the first of many moments that would move both speaker and audience over the next hour. Sendak's speech, thoughtful and eloquent, will be published in due course, but let me offer a few personal impressions from the vantage of my second-row seat.

First is the sense of valediction, of, as Somerset Maugham put it, "Summing Up" that overlay Sendak's speech. It was evident in the attention he gave to his "many mentors," to the early editors and librarians whom he called "the great giant ladies," and to his "best mama and papa," author Ruth Kraus and her artist-husband Crockett Johnson. It was evident in the many haunting phrases that peppered his remarks about the evolution of his career, phrases like "fidelity to the real child," "the determination to tell the truth," "the incoherence of the creative act," and "how to focus the creative self." And it was evident in the very title he had selected for his speech. "Descent into Limbo" expressed his feeling, Sendak explained, that he had been "in one form of limbo or other all [his] life," starting with childhood memories of a near-fatal bout with scarlet fever, the kidnapping of the Lindbergh baby, and the Great Depression and continuing into a midlife and mid-career limbo that began when he turned fifty and ended only when he began a second career designing operas.

And, yes, he had some salty things to say about the limbo of contemporary publishing, which he called "Conglomerateland" with its "minefield of 'bottom line' mines." But ultimately it was childhood, which he called "the armature of all my work," that provided the most moving and memorable moments of the afternoon when, near the end of his speech, he departed from his prepared text to recall Rosie, his childhood neighbor who became the model for all the kids in his work, and another little girl—this one nameless—whom he encountered later in his life when he toured the cancer ward of a British hospital.

Children at risk brought him back to his text and to comments on his current project, *Brundibar,* which he feels has brought his life full circle. For this children's opera, with its inextricable links to the Terezin (Theresienstadt) concentration camp, reminds him of "all the murdered Jews who haunted my childhood," specters that surely inspired his lifelong feeling of "an implied mission" in his work "to save the children who survived the Second World War and the Holocaust."

It is the kind of work that Keats called "soul-making," and it may explain why Sendak ended with an observation that seemed almost to surprise him: "I am," he concluded, "strangely content."

One hopes he is. For anyone whose work is informed by what Gregory Maguire had earlier that day called "a bedrock belief that the weak and lowly are not to be abused" deserves to be.

Or so it seems to me.

May 15, 2003 • *Booklist*

Love, Passion, and Lectures

THERE'S GOOD NEWS from America's Heartland: the University of Wisconsin–Madison has announced the establishment of an annual lecture and award named in honor of Charlotte Zolotow, who attended the university on a writing scholarship from 1933 to 1936. She went on, of course, to become one of the most distinguished editors and publishers in the history of books for young readers. Her association with Harper Junior Books began in 1938 when she went to work as editorial assistant to children's book editor Ursula Nordstrom. Six years later, with the publication of *The Park Book*, she began a second career as a writer. Thereafter, her two book-centered lives evolved simultaneously. For in addition to producing a growing body of poetic, sensitive, and innovative picture books, she continued to advance editorially at Harper, becoming, in turn, senior editor, editorial director, associate publisher, and vice-president. By the time I met her in 1986, she had been with the company for forty-eight years and had become the editor of her own imprint, Charlotte Zolotow Books. By then she had also written more than sixty titles of her own, including such classics as *Mr. Rabbit and the Lovely Present*, *William's Doll*, and *My Grandson Lew*.

The occasion for our meeting was something called the Third Pacific Rim Conference in Children's Literature, held at UCLA. I was a member of the conference's board of directors, and Charlotte was one of our distinguished speakers and, additionally, had agreed to be a guest on my television author-interview program *In Print*. I was understandably nervous about meeting and interviewing someone of her stature, but I quickly discovered that she had a gift for putting the anxious at ease and a smile that made anyone who saw it glad to be alive. Though she was always affable and soft-spoken, it quickly became obvious when she began talking about the editing and writing of books why she had chosen to title her conference speech "Passion in Publishing."

"Love and passion are a large part of being an editor," she told her rapt audience; "not love of the individual person who is writing, but love of his talent. It is the duty of the publisher to encourage not only the authors whom we do publish but anyone who has some spark that burns underneath even the unsuccessful attempts."

I was among those she encouraged, as a matter of fact, and I will always be grateful for that. And it's one final reason why I'm so delighted that through the establishment of the Charlotte Zolotow Lecture and Award, this remarkable woman's dedication to excellence will continue to encourage others. By the time you read this, the first award will have been presented to Vera B. Williams, author of *Lucky Song*, and the first lecture will have been delivered by Karla Kuskin, recipient of the National Council of Teachers of English Award for Excellence in Poetry in 1979.

With the establishment of this annual lecture, Charlotte Zolotow joins a select company of other literary leaders whose names have similar lectureships: May Hill Arbuthnot, Zena Sutherland, Anne Carroll Moore, and Francis Clarke Sayers.

In their lives and their work, these five luminaries accomplished (and, in the cases of Charlotte and Zena, continue to accomplish) something that most of us can only aspire to: making a difference. Thanks to their passion for writing and publishing, their tireless commitment to kids and reading, and their courageous advocacy of excellence in literature, the lives of generations of young people have been changed for the better, not to mention the generations of librarians and educators who have been inspired to professional excellence by their example.

Establishing lectures in their names is not only a tribute to accomplishment, but also a wonderful way of continuing a great tradition of learning. Through lectures, new generations of students, librarians, and teachers are given opportunities to hear, learn from, and meet other great names in children's and young adult literature. Since its establishment in 1993, for example, UCLA's Sayers Lecture has brought Margaret McElderry, Ashley Bryan, Katherine Paterson, Lois Lowry, and Robert Cormier to its southern California campus.

Of course, what May Hill Arbuthnot said of the establishment in 1969 of the lectureship that bears her name—"It means we shall be hearing new voices speak with new insight and new emphasis"—could be applied to any of the others, too. In their respective ways, they focus our attention on present conditions and offer an informed prognosis for the future.

But they also offer a passport to what Charlotte Zolotow has memorably called "that foreign country, the past."

They remind us of our roots and of how they were nourished by a lovely kind of baton-passing continuity that may no longer exist in the hyperkinetic, flux-filled world of today. I love thinking of the connections that linked these five professional lives. Consider that Charlotte Zolotow, one of the century's most distinguished editors, began her career working with another such, Ursula Nordstrom. Or consider that Anne Carroll Moore "invented" children's book reviewing in her 1920s "Three Owls" column, which appeared in *The Bookman*, while Zena Sutherland refined the form to an art in her many years as editor of *The Bulletin of the Center for Children's Books*. Or consider May Hill Arbuthnot's contribution as the author of one of the century's most influential textbooks, *Children and Books*, and the fact that it was, yes, Zena Sutherland who undertook its editorship in later editions. Or consider that Moore, one of the century's most influential children's librarians as head of children's work for the New York Public Library, hired Frances Clarke Sayers who, years later, would not only succeed her but would also become her biographer. Or consider the academic contributions of Arbuthnot at Case Western Reserve, Sutherland at the University of Chicago, and Sayers at UCLA.

I'm not trying to forge some kind of biblical chain of "begats" with such observations; each of these remarkable women remains sui generis, but their lives have been so linked by accomplishment that I think it's wonderfully appropriate that their names should also be linked, celebrated, and perpetuated in lectureships. Zena Sutherland's description of May Hill Arbuthnot as "a wise and blithe spirit who has made a permanent and significant contribution to children's literature" might equally well be applied to all of these extraordinary women.

The world has become so complex that I'm not sure if it's any longer possible for individuals to make such life-changing differences. If that is so, it is all the more reason to treasure and honor the names of those who have.

November 15, 1998 • *Booklist*

Remembering Myra and Mike

HISTORY WILL RECORD that libraries, literature, and young readers have recently lost two exemplary leaders, Myra Cohn Livingston and Mike Printz. But in more immediate and personal terms, all of us who knew them have lost two of our best friends.

Although they never met each other, Myra and Mike had much in common: a passion for words; a single-minded devotion to libraries, books, and reading; a love for teaching and those they taught; and an extraordinary capacity for friendship. Myra, who died on August 23, left three children—now gifted adults—a large house in a canyon above Beverly Hills that was filled with wonderful books (she was an avid collector), and also another enduring book-related legacy: the eighty-three volumes of poetry she either wrote or edited. It is perhaps no surprise that the music of language should have come so naturally to her ear and imagination, since she was a gifted musician, a French horn player who studied with Darius Milhaud and performed with the California Junior Symphony Orchestra. Her first book, *Whispers and Other Poems,* was written when she was a student at Sarah Lawrence and was published in 1958 by Margaret McElderry, who was her editor for nearly forty years. As a poet, anthologist, and editor herself, Myra won a clutch of glittering literary prizes, including the National Council of Teachers of English (NCTE) Award for Excellence in Poetry. When I first met her in 1976, I was amazed that this elegant, worldly, accomplished woman could write so insightfully and authentically about childhood, often in the very voice of a child. To that point, she once said, "I am not consciously aware of writing for children; my poetry seems to be born of the genre of childhood. . . . I feel I have never departed from the child I was; the child I knew best." Children were important to her; the joy of her life was her grandson, and her last book, *B Is for Baby* (McElderry, 1996), celebrates him. Also important to her, though, was her teaching. She conducted a master class in poetry at UCLA from 1973 until her death. And she was as devoted to her students as they were to her. The day I was interviewing her for the column "The Poet's Question," the phone rang; it was one of those students calling with the news that her first book had just been accepted for publication. Though by that time I had known Myra for nearly twenty years, I had never seen her so elated, so spontaneously happy for the good fortune of another; she looked like a child who has just opened the most wonderful present imaginable. It was a gift to me, too: the best possible way to remember a gloriously talented and generous-spirited friend.

I was privileged to be present at a similarly defining moment in Mike Printz's life. Following the 1993 ALA Midwinter Meeting, I flew to Kansas to visit Mike at his home in Topeka. As my good luck would have it, we were sitting in his kitchen drinking coffee one morning when the phone rang; the caller was conveying the news that Mike had been named winner of that year's Grolier Award. "Well, bless your heart," Mike told the caller, and when he hung up the phone, we both got out our handkerchiefs for some necessary nose-blowing and eye-wiping. Mike wore his sentimental heart on his sleeve—a trait we shared in common; like Bill Clinton, Mike and I could cry at the opening of a car wash!

Life is an exercise in irony. Consider how ironic it is that Mike's life should have been ended by heart problems, since he had not only the softest but the best heart of anybody I ever knew—the largest, the kindest, the most considerate and compassionate. For my part, I give heartfelt thanks that I had the privilege of his friendship. Mike believed in friendship, and he believed in his friends; he had more confidence in their abilities than they sometimes did themselves. He was positive, for example, that I was capable of becoming a YALSA board member, and two years after I did, he was positive that I was up to the ordeal (he called it an "opportunity") of serving as the division's vice-president–president elect. I was hardly the only one, though, whose professional life was changed by Mike's belief in his friends' abilities. So it's not at all ironic but, instead, appropriate that the news of his death on September 27 should have arrived during a YALSA Executive Board meeting and that four of the five of us present acknowledged that we were there because of Mike's example, urging, and influence.

Mike loved his friends, and, like Myra, he loved his students. They loved him, too. The Grolier Award acknowledged his tireless work to give his kids unusual educational opportunities. The author-in-residence program he started at Topeka West High School, where he was librarian for twenty-nine years, brought America's leading young adult authors there not only to lecture but to work with the students in creative writing workshops. Mike was also a pioneer in oral history, and when he retired in 1993, a reunion of his oral-history students was held at the Kansas Museum of History. A picture of Mike, surrounded by a sea of former students who had traveled from all over America to honor him on that occasion, hung on the wall across from his desk.

Like Myra, Mike loved books. The author Gary Paulsen recalled watching Mike holding one: "He smiled down at the book and petted it with his right hand, the way he would pet a puppy or touch a friend. I thought then of what a wonderful thing that is—to love a book so much that you can pet it, seek solace from it, view it as a friend." And like Myra, Mike loved language. He was especially fond of regional talk and the now-forgotten turns of phrase that colored local conversation when he was a boy growing up in small-town Kansas; knowing that I shared this interest, he would often call me to ask if I were familiar with a phrase whose meaning temporarily eluded him (the most recent was "butter and egg man"). He still subscribed to the weekly newspaper that chronicled daily doings in his tiny hometown and delighted in finding small stories that unintentionally brought large laughs; he loved reading these to me verbatim; his (and my) favorite was the report of a local reception where the hostess, caught shorthanded at the last moment, rose to the occasion at the refreshment table, where, as the paper innocently put it, she "poured from both ends." Mike also loved quotations, especially ones from Saint Jerome, the patron saint of libraries; however, once when he must have had a particularly trying day at Topeka West, Mike sent along a quote from the Koran, instead: "Let no profane one enter here." He tartly added, "That would cut my attendance down to a handful!" Perhaps it's appropriate, therefore, that my first thought when I heard the news of Mike's untimely passing was a quotation; here it is (I've taken the liberty of correcting Shakespeare's misspelling of the most important word)—"Good night, sweet Printz; And flights of angels sing thee to thy rest."

November 15, 1996 • *Booklist*

Remembering Bill

I SUPPOSE THAT every life has its share of sorrows and satisfactions. One of the sorrows of my life, for example, is that I never got to meet Walter R. Brooks, author of my beloved Freddy the Pig books. On the other hand, one of the satisfactions (though that seems too slight a word to describe it) is that I *did* get to meet Bill Morris or, more formally, William C. Morris, vice-president and director of library promotion at HarperCollins Children's Books, who died on September 29. Even more satisfying, I had the privilege of becoming his friend—or at least I flatter myself that I did.

I first met Bill some twenty years ago—and in the best way imaginable. I was introduced to him by Charlotte Zolotow, celebrated author and then head of children's publishing at Harper. The occasion was an unforgettable—for me, at least—lunch the three of us shared in New York, which was, quintessentially, Bill's town. Though he was born in Eagle Pass, Texas, his true home was Manhattan, the only place he could ever contemplate living. No matter where he traveled, he insisted on having the *New York Times* delivered to his hotel room each morning, and on the rare occasions when that wasn't possible, he was bereft—or at least grouchy all day! Yes, he could be a bit grouchy and also wonderfully wry and irreverent when he was among friends. But he was also unfailingly kind, considerate, thoughtful, generous, gallant, and gentlemanly. I adored the man, but—file this under the "Sorrows" heading—I was never able to tell him so, because of the natural reserve he always wore like those ever-elegant neckties, which seemed a sort of sartorial shorthand for his innate good taste and sophistication. An intensely private man—almost no one knew how seriously ill he was, for example, until very near the end—he was chary of expressed emotions and so whenever he spoke of something deeply meaningful to him, he did so casually, almost jokingly. For example, whenever we spoke on the phone, and I would ask what he had been up to, his reply, inevitably, was an offhand, "Oh, I've been busy saving the children of America."

We would laugh at that, but I soon realized that he wasn't really joking; on the contrary, he was sharing a fundamental part of himself with me: his deep-seated love of children's literature, his encyclopedic knowledge of it, and his corollary belief in its artful power to save lives. Since we shared that belief, it quickly became a bond between us.

Bill loved discovering new talent and telling others about it in wonderfully creative ways. Of course, that was his work: he was a marketer par excellence, and he had begun his career at Harper in 1955 as a salesman. But he became vastly more. It is no exaggeration to say that Bill, as Eden Ross Lipson wrote in her *New York Times* obituary, "is often credited with developing the modern marketing of children's books."

But for this wonderful man, marketing was more than simply flogging merchandise. It was sharing his absolutely authentic enthusiasm. And he was a genius at bringing books and people together. It was through him that I was introduced to the work of Francesca Lia Block, Bruce Brooks, Chris Lynch, William Joyce, Terry Trueman, and so many others. I quickly learned that he had flawless taste, and I can honestly say I was never disappointed by one of his recommendations.

And I can also honestly say I cannot imagine a publishing world without him. Few of us can. That became obvious at ALA's recent Annual Conference in Toronto, where the strangest thing about a very strange convention was Bill's absence from it. Everyone missed him, for it was the first time in our collective memory that Bill had not been in attendance. I knew he hadn't been feeling well—I had seen him in New York several months before, and he had called me only days before Toronto to tell me that he just didn't feel up to going—but still nothing could have prepared me for the oddness of an ALA without Bill. For one thing, we always had dinner together at the ALA conference, just the two of us, a tradition I treasured. But it was more than that. And it was linked to the reason it is so hard for me to accept his passing. See, here's the thing of it: Bill was simply the best. He was a nonpareil. He embodied integrity and high standards and a commitment to excellence. No wonder he was the first recipient of the Association for Library Service to Children's (ALSC) Distinguished Service Award. So when he left us, more than a man died; a standard of excellence died, too, and I fear that a way of life, a history, a tradition also went with him. Bill was one of the last links to a publishing world that existed before the bottom line became such an overriding consideration, before publishing became an international exercise in info- and edu-tainment, before it became so conglomeratized that nothing but size seems to matter.

When I first met Bill, individuals still mattered and still could make a difference. Indeed, both he and Charlotte had made such a difference that they were already legendary in children's publishing. And there I was, having lunch with them. Yikes! Oh sure, I was by that time director of the

Beverly Hills Public Library and had a small reputation as a reviewer, but inside, where it mattered, I was still a timid teenager from Logansport, Indiana, and I was terrified they would find me to be a fraud.

Well, if they did, they didn't let on. On the contrary, they were the first people ever to suggest I should consider becoming a full-time writer. And in due course, Charlotte offered me my first book contract, and Bill became a staunch advocate of my work even when I began publishing books with, well, other houses (Bill was first, last, and always a Harper man).

Sadly, Charlotte retired before Harper published my first book, but Bill remained; indeed, he could not contemplate a life of retirement. "What would I do?" he asked every time I suggested, years later, that he might enjoy slowing down a bit. So, in a sense, I suppose, it's a blessing that he was able to work until the end. But it makes the transition to a world without him that much harder, and the unexpected suddenness of his passing that much more difficult.

But how deeply satisfying it is to have had the privilege of knowing him.

And here's one more satisfaction, though I know Bill would wince at my sharing it: the last time I saw him was for dinner—in New York, of course. As we were leaving the restaurant, I did something that was—for me—wildly uncharacteristic. I impulsively hugged him. Of course, I almost put my eye out on the cigarette he was lighting (he smoked, you know). But even if I had, it would have been worth it. It was a satisfyingly spontaneous way of showing him my gratitude for all that he had done for me—and for the children of America!

We thank you, Bill. And we will always remember you.

November 15, 2003 • *Booklist*

His First Novel

HE WROTE HIS first novel for children one hot, lonely summer in Washington, DC, where he was working for the American Red Cross. He wrote it, he later recalled, for his own amusement, but, as often happens when an author writes just to amuse himself, the result amused others as well—whole generations of others.

In fact, by the time you read this, a multi-generational number of those amused readers will have completed a four-day pilgrimage to his birthplace, Rome, New York, where they gathered from October 29 through November 1 to celebrate him, his work, and the twentieth anniversary of the founding of the international fan club that is dedicated to the preservation and perpetuation of his writings and of his literary alter ego, a pig named Freddy.

Yes, the author was Walter R. Brooks and his first novel for children was, of course, *To and Again,* published in 1927 by Alfred A. Knopf and later retitled *Freddy Goes to Florida.*

I was all of eight when I first encountered Walter's immortal creation. That I still remember my first meeting with Freddy says something important about the intensity of my lifelong love affair with . . . that pig.

The encounter took place in the third-grade classroom at McKinley Elementary School, which was located in a quiet, leafy neighborhood on the north side of my hometown, Logansport, Indiana. I was actually a second-grader at the time, but along with a handful of other "accelerated" students, I joined the third-graders for reading instruction. To this day, I remember opening the pages of my classroom reader (*On Longer Trails* by Gates, Huber, Peardon, and Salisbury, a quartet of names that sounded like one of the law firms on Fourth Street across from the courthouse in downtown Logansport) and finding there a story called "Adventure in a Swamp." It was, I discovered, a real page-turner about a group of funny animals from somewhere in New York state who were, of all things, vacationing in Florida, where they became embroiled in a bone-chilling encounter—not with a hurricane but, instead, with an assortment of alligators, the most sinister of which, the Grandfather of All the Alligators, had a smile "nine feet wide."

Wow! This was great stuff, lots more exciting than the stories that surrounded it: the wimpy "Jim Jolly and His Friends" and the dreary "Early Days in Our Country—Building Homes."

I'm sure my breath was bated as I read how the animals bested the denizens of the swamp—not by blowing them away with a battery of howitzers as they might today, but by using their wits, instead!

End of story and end, or so I then thought, of my experience with these animals: Freddy the pig, Jinx the cat, Mrs. Wiggins the cow, and Charles the henpecked rooster and his acerbic wife, Henrietta.

Fate would have it otherwise, however, for it was only a few days later that, browsing the children's stacks in the Logansport Public Library, I came across a whole shelf full of books that, thanks to their similarity of design, I recognized as a series! I loved series, having cut my eyeteeth on the Thornton W. Burgess Bedtime Story Books and the Oz books, and I was always on the lookout for more. Eagerly, I pulled a title at random from the shelf, opened it, and discovered—Oh my God!—that it was a *whole book* about those funny farm animals. In fact, it was the very book from which the story in my reader had been excerpted. And not only was there more to the story of the intrepid animals' trip to the Sunshine State, there was a whole shelf of other books about them, too! Be still, my palpitating, pre-adolescent heart!

It wasn't until years later that I would discover, from talking with fellow members of the Friends of Freddy, that countless others had experienced similar childhood scenes of passionate and life-changing discovery. The Canadian playwright Dave Carley, who founded the Friends of Freddy back in 1984, recalls Saturdays at the Peterborough Public Library when "a young tough boy" (Dave's older brother) "held back throngs of eager readers at the door, while the tough's skinny but fleet-footed brother" (that would be Dave) "ran upstairs and hogged the best available Freddys for yet another week. Demand was great in those days, and the library had imposed a diet of two Freddys per week per skinny boy."

No matter how many Freddys one could borrow, however, each one was a feast for the imagination and, as it has turned out, a banquet for budding writers everywhere. Freddy was himself a writer—a newspaper editor and poet whose example and omnivorous appetite for words seem to have inspired an extraordinary number of his youthful fans to choose the writer's life for themselves. Just consider that the founder of the Friends of Freddy is a playwright; the secretary-treasurer worked for years in publishing; the only two-term past president (that would be me) is writing these words; the current co-presidents are, respectively, a publisher and a graphic novelist; "celebrity" fans include the likes of Lorne Michaels (TV writer-producer), Henry Cooper (former *New Yorker* aerospace writer), Tony Hiss (another

New Yorker writer), Larry Yep (noted children's book author), and . . . well, the list goes on and on like the open road that Freddy celebrated in song: "Oh, the winding road is long, is long // But never too long for me."

You see, Freddy was not only a writer but also an inveterate—and intrepid—traveler who often wrote about the lure of the faraway and the roads that took you there. Here's another example: "Oh, it's over the hill and down the road // And we'll borrow the moon for a light // And wherever we go, one thing we know: The road will lead us right."

Walter R. Brooks led his readers right, too—not only in his first novel for kids but in the 24 others that would follow over the course of the next 31 years. His words were roads that led his readers to a land where the scenery may have been familiar—rural and small-town America in the earlier years of the twentieth century—but where the language was definitely exotic, where sentences were studded with such words as *caravansary, predilection, skulduggery,* even *sesquipedalianism,* for heaven's sake!

The Freddy books were treasure troves of odd, unusual, polysyllabic words, words that so excited the curiosity and enriched the vocabularies of their readers that it is no wonder at all that so many of them grew up to choose words as their own life's work.

And that, as Freddy might have said (but mercifully didn't), is no hogwash!

November 15, 2004 • *Booklist*

Hog Heaven

I HAVE THIS wonderful recurring dream in which I discover a Freddy the Pig book that I've never read. Or if the dream weaver is working overtime, it's a whole *shelf* of new "Freddies" that I discover! But whether it's one title or many, my emotion in the dream is always the same: it's precisely that thrill of anticipation and discovery that I experienced as a ten-year-old racing home from Columbia Elementary School to discover in the mailbox the package I'd been waiting for. The package from Kroch's & Brentano's Bookstore in Chicago; the package containing the new Freddy book I'd ordered a week or two before! Oh the joy, oh the rapture! For as long as the dream—and that vividly resurrected rush of emotion—lasts, I'm in hog heaven!

But then, too soon, I wake up to the hellish reality that there are no new Freddy books and never will be again. The man who wrote them, Walter R. Brooks, died in 1958, and I know from my personal investigation (Freddy's not the only one who is a detective) that no unpublished stories about the pig nonpareil survived him. Too bad, eh?

But wait! I have another recurring dream: in this one, I discover that the Freddy books, all 26 of them, are coming back into print after languishing in publishing limbo for—in the case of some of the titles—more than 30 years.

And now—oh, be still, my heart—*this* dream is coming true at last. Peter Mayer's Overlook Press has just reissued facsimile editions of the first and third titles in the series—*Freddy Goes to Florida* (coincidentally, the first Freddy book I ever read) and *Freddy the Detective*. But wait—here's the really big news: Overlook plans to continue reissuing titles until the whole Freddy saga is back in print. Oh, glory hallelujah!

How did this unreachable dream turn into reality? Meet Wray and Loni Romiger, owners of the Purple Mountain Press. Located in the Catskills village of Fleischmanns, New York, Purple Mountain publishes regional books about New York state. In addition to being publishers, the Romigers are—no surprise—stalwart members of Friends of Freddy, the international Freddy the Pig fan club. And, as it turns out, they're also longtime acquaintances of the publisher Peter Mayer.

Wray recalls, "My wife Loni and I met Peter Mayer about twenty-five years ago. We had just started a small printing business in the Catskills, and we dreamed of publishing books someday. A mutual friend brought Peter to our shop. He was looking for a local printer to produce catalogs for the

Overlook Press, a publishing company he had recently founded with his father in Woodstock."

It was at another meeting of Wray, Loni, and Peter, twenty-something years later, this time a chance encounter at a publishing party, when the dream began to turn into reality. For it was at this meeting that Mayer told the Romigers of his plans to retire as head of Penguin Books to devote himself full time to the Overlook Press.

Nothing was said about the out-of-print pig at that meeting, but it wasn't long thereafter when it occurred to Wray that, given the economics of contemporary publishing, a smaller house with national distribution like the Overlook Press would be the ideal publisher to rescue Freddy from out-of-print oblivion.

"I sat down," Wray says, "and carefully composed a two-page letter to Peter laying out my case. It took many months before my letter reached him as he circled the globe on behalf of Penguin. But early one Saturday morning in October 1996, he called."

"The Freddy books? Of course I'll publish the Freddy books. I thought I was the only one who still cares for them."

As for me: I suspected something was up when an obviously very excited Loni called me later that same day to tell me that Wray would be phoning me that evening with some very important news. Would I be home?

Would I!

And yes, that evening I heard the good news from Wray, and, less than two weeks later, I found myself talking with Peter Mayer himself at the biennial Friends of Freddy Conference in Cooperstown, New York. We talked about the historic importance of the Freddy books in the evolution of humor in American children's literature, and, to my delight, I learned that Mayer had been an avid Freddy reader as a boy—just like me.

The rest, as they say, is history. And now, seventeen months later as I write this, there on the desk at my elbow (right next to a framed picture of Walter R. Brooks cocking an ironic eyebrow) are copies of *Freddy Goes to Florida* and *Freddy the Detective*—faithful facsimiles of the original titles published by Alfred A. Knopf in 1927 and 1932, respectively. Oh, the trim size is a tad smaller—publishing economics again—and on the verso of the title page are words that didn't appear in the originals: encomia from a number of magazines and newspapers singing the latter-day praises of the pig o' my heart. But otherwise, the books look almost exactly as they did in their original editions, the ones I know from my childhood.

Ah, yes—there is another small difference. On the back of the dust jacket appear a few words of praise from Michael Cart. That's me, Mom. Here's what I say: "The Freddy books are authentic American classics. Filled with wonderful wordplay, memorable characters, enduring friendships, and laugh-out-loud good humor, they are timeless, as readable and enjoyable today as when they were first published."

I look at these words, and I see my name printed next to them on the dust jackets of these two Freddy the Pig books, and I wonder. I wonder what I would have thought forty-six years ago when I was a ten-year-old boy, running on my heart-pounding way home to check the mailbox at 1319 Sycamore Street to see if my dreams had come true, and the latest Freddy book had arrived for me to read. What would I have thought if I could have seen into the future and known that, one day four decades later, my own name would appear on the dust jacket of a Freddy book—a book rescued from oblivion so that whole new generations of kids like me could meet the fictional character who became my best friend and may, perhaps, become theirs, too?

What would I have thought?

"I'm in hog heaven." That's what I would have thought.

Thanks to Peter Mayer and to Wray and Loni Romiger for making it possible.

It's a dream come true.

March 15, 1998 • *Booklist*

America's New Laureate

IN MID-JUNE, Librarian of Congress James Billington named 77-year-old Donald Hall to be America's fourteenth poet laureate. If you think, as I do, that being appointed poet laureate is a big deal, then this is cause for celebration, since Hall has long been one of America's finest—and one of my favorite—writers. In fact, I devoted my very first Carte Blanche column to him and his work way back in June 1994. I remember that I had just finished reading his illuminating memoir *Life Work* (Beacon, 1993) and was captivated by his thoughts on the writer's life.

"I stay home," he observed, "and write poems—and essays, stories, textbooks, children's books, biography . . . Work? Work. I make my living at it."

Since I also stay home and write for a living, I can identify with this, though I'm nowhere near as successful or as talented as Hall. And if you held my feet to the fire, I'd probably admit that I find the writing process a wee bit more onerous than he does. Because it's clear that for him such "work" is a labor of love, and all of his writing evidences the truth of his own later observation, "Everybody writes best out of obsession or love."

His several obsessions—baseball (he's a devoted Boston Red Sox fan), poetry, his family, and especially New Hampshire and the ancient farm on Eagle Pond where he lives in the shadow of Ragged Mountain—have all provided recurring and much-loved subjects for his best work and in so many literary forms that he has been called "one of the most thorough literary professionals in America."

Thorough and productive! In addition to 18 volumes of poetry, his oeuvre also includes 20 prose works and a dozen children's books, including *Ox-Cart Man,* whose illustrator, Barbara Cooney, received the 1980 Caldecott Medal for her beautifully realized depictions of this timeless story.

In the afterword to his 1995 essay collection, *Principal Products of Portugal,* Hall shares two secrets of freelancing that involve *Ox-Cart Man.* "One," he says, "is to sell everything as many times as you can. Another is to listen. My cousin Paul Fenton told me the story of the ox-cart man, which became a poem, a children's book, and a paragraph in an essay. At store, post office, and church, I keep my eyes and ears open."

He learned to listen from his maternal grandfather, Wesley Wells, in whose white clapboard farmhouse he has lived since 1975. In a sublime essay Hall wrote for *Newsweek* magazine (April 15, 1985), and which should be required reading for everyone who loves the sound of language, he recalled his grandfather's habit of reciting poetry while he worked around the farm. "His hands stripped milk to the poem's beat. He threw back his head, rolled his eyes in high drama and pounded out: 'But there is no joy in Mudville—mighty Casey has struck out.'"

As a boy, Hall visited his grandfather every summer and—perhaps from hearing these exuberant recitations—knew by the time he was fourteen that he wanted to be a poet. And now, sixty-three years later, he is America's poet, our laureate. What are his plans for a post that has no specific duties?

"It's an opportunity to plug poetry," he told the *Washington Post* (June 14, 2006). He is intrigued by the possibility of starting a poetry channel on one of the satellite radio networks or of urging National Public Radio to pay more attention to poetry. Or he might follow the lead of his immediate predecessor, Nebraskan Ted Kooser, who had a syndicated weekly newspaper column, or of Kooser's predecessor, Billy Collins, who started a highly regarded project that urged school administrators to include a poem in their daily public announcements.

Perhaps because of such efforts by previous laureates, Hall told *Newsweek*, "poetry is a lot more important now than it's ever been in this country. There are many more magazines, many more publishers."

And—I might interpose—more than a few of them are publishing extraordinary work for young adults by such gifted poets as Sonya Sones, Helen Frost, Marilyn Nelson, Paul B. Janeczko, Naomi Shihab Nye, Nikki Grimes, and others.

Hall's selection as poet laureate is also especially felicitous at a time of increasing challenge to freedom of speech. For Hall has "a record of being very courageous in talking about freedom of expression," according to former laureate Robert Pinsky. Hall served on the advisory council for the National Endowment for the Arts in the early 1990s and was refreshingly blunt in his public criticism of those whom he called "bullies and art bashers." The years since then apparently have not mellowed him, since he recently promised the *New York Times*, "If I see First Amendment violations, I will speak up."

Speaking up and speaking out brings me back to Hall's *Newsweek* essay, which was titled "Bring Back the Out-Loud Culture." It celebrated not only Hall's much-loved, poetry-reciting grandfather but also a way of life, a culture that he and others of his generation embraced. "Before the late 1920s and 1930s, American culture was *out-loud*," he wrote, noting that "public recitations and performances were at the center of American culture."

"We continually turned print into sound. But when we stopped memorizing and reciting literature, our ability to read started its famous decline. In order to become a nation of readers," Hall concluded, "we need again to become a nation of reciters."

Perhaps making that need a reality could be his contribution as poet laureate. Until then, I will continue to do my bit by reading Hall's words out loud to anyone who will listen, for I continue to find them among the sweetest, sanest, and most satisfying I know.

August, 2006 • *Booklist*

Thanks for joining me in this survey of twenty-three years of columns. I hope you've had as good a time as I have along the way. But now you must excuse me. It's time to write my next column, the first one of the next twenty-three years . . .

CONCLUSION

Some Stray Thoughts on Columns

ACCORDING TO MY *Webster's New World Dictionary,* a column—aside from being an architectural feature, duh—is "any of a series of feature articles appearing regularly in a newspaper or magazine by a particular author or about a certain subject."

Why the specific word *column,* though? My dictionary—like a hyper-caffeinated Lochinvar—once again comes galloping to the rescue: **column:** "any," it says, "of the vertical sections of printed matter that are side by side on a page, separated by a rule or blank space."

So originally (though don't ask me how long ago originally was) a column was a feature article that filled a column of type in a newspaper or magazine. Columns still often fill a, well, column. I just found one by Nicholas Kristof that appeared in the *New York Times* for March 19, 2017. If you're curious (I was) as to how many words such a column contains, I did a hasty estimate that came in at 1,030 words or eighteen column inches, which is about par for the course, because most columns are said to be 1,000–1,200 words long (mine come in at a uniform 1,000). So length is one thing, then, that most columns have in common. What are some others? Well, they appear regularly; and so they're not occasional pieces like essays, but features that are published according to a predictable schedule that readers can count on; thus, Carte Blanche appears monthly, while Kristof's column appears twice a week. The late, legendary Jimmy Breslin's column appeared three times a week. Columns are by the same author—Michael Cart or Nicholas Kristof or Jimmy Breslin—and focus on, generally speaking, similar topics. For example, mine are all related in one way or another to books, reading, writing, or publishing. Kristof's are usually—though not always—about international problems and issues; his March 19 column focused on the impact of President Trump's proposed budget on hunger in Africa and the Middle East. Breslin's columns were usually about New York eccentrics in the style of Damon Runyon. And, finally, columns often contain the author's opinions (Kristof, for example, argues that the president's budget is wrongheaded because it cuts or eliminates U.S. aid to impacted African and Middle Eastern countries). My own columns regularly feature my own opinions, too, especially when, for example, I evaluate books or select the best ones of the year.

At the risk of oversimplification, many columns can be put into five topical categories: Political (in addition to Kristof, how about Paul Krugman and Gail Collins, also of the *New York Times*?); Sports (young adult novelist Robert Lipsyte wrote a celebrated *New York Times* sports column for a number of years); Advice ("Dear Abby" and "Ann Landers," of course); Humor (Dave Barry anyone?); and Local (my local newspaper, the *Columbus* (IN) *Republic,* for example, features a regular column on local history).

Columns are also typically as ephemeral as the publications—newspapers and magazines again—that contain them. Ephemeral, that is, until some enlightened someone decides to collect them and publish them in a book—like this one, for example!

There are exceptions to the rule of ephemera. In 2011 John Avon, senior political columnist of *Newsweek,* conducted a national survey of columnists to determine the ten best American columns in history; in other words, ones of enduring interest. Here they are:

1. Ernie Pyle. "The Death of Captain Waskow." Scripps Howard. 1/10/1944.
2. Francis Church. "Yes, Virginia, There Is a Santa Claus." *New York Sun.* 9/21/1897.
3. Molly Ivins. "A Short Story about the Vietnam War Memorial." *Dallas Times Herald.* 11/30/1982.
4. Westbrook Pegler. "The Death of Frankie Jerome." News Syndicate. 1/18/1924.
5. Jimmy Breslin. "It's an Honor." *New York Herald Tribune.* 11/26/1963.
6. Leonard Pitts, Jr. "We'll Go Forward from This Moment." *The Miami Herald.* 9/11/2001.
7. Murray Kempton. "He Went All the Way." *New York Post.* 9/22/1958.
8. Dave Barry. "Pithy into the Wind." *The Miami Herald.* 3/20/1987.
9. Mike Royko. "Daley Embodied Chicago." *Chicago Sun Times.* 12/21/1976.
10. H. L. Mencken. "Gamalielese." *Baltimore Sun.* 3/7/1921.

No, Virginia, a Carte Blanche column didn't make the list. Perhaps another time . . .

Aside from a paycheck, what motivates a writer to do a column? Breslin once said, "Rage is the only quality which has kept me, or anybody I have ever studied, writing columns for newspapers." Does rage motivate me, then? In a word, "no." I'm not quite sure what does motivate me, though. Curiosity, perhaps? I long ago discovered that the best way to learn about a subject is to write about it; that certainly motivated me to write my critical history of young adult literature, *Young Adult Literature: From Romance to Realism* (now in its third edition from ALA's Neal-Schuman imprint). That book, of course, involved a near surfeit of research, a process I dote upon; my columns obviously require far less digging, alas, though I'm often driven to my reference books to do background checks or confirm facts.

Among the many challenges confronting the columnist, the first is finding a subject for the column; in other words what is it to be about? In Breslin's *New York Times* obituary Dan Barry wrote: "Mr. Breslin began his day early, making calls to judges, politicians, police officers and other journalists, always greeting them with words that signaled he was in the hunt for news: 'What's doin'?"

"He just keeps calling until he has a column in his head," his second wife explained. As for me: my ideas seldom—if ever—begin with a phone call. Instead, they begin with the spotlight focus of the issue of *Booklist* at which the column is targeted. Accordingly, my column about my personal environment, that is, the interior of my house, appeared in the issue with the spotlight on "Sustainability." In another issue, with the spotlight on "Crafts and Hobbies," I wrote about book collecting. You get the idea.

Among other challenges encountered in writing columns, one certainly is the fact that they are deadline-driven. I can't imagine the pressure involved in writing a weekly or twice-weekly or thrice-weekly column. Writing a monthly column puts quite enough pressure on me, thank you very much. The one good thing about deadline pressure is that it focuses the mind wonderfully, as—Dr. Johnson once opined—does the prospect of being hanged on the morrow. As for me, I do often find myself writing a column the day before it is due. I clear the decks so that I have the entire day in which to write it, though once I have the idea for the column, I can generally write it in a morning. My most imperative deadline came not in the case of a column but an essay review, though. Some years ago I was retained by the *Los Angeles Times* to write a 1,000-word review of the fifth Harry Potter book, *Harry*

Potter and the Order of the Phoenix. I was given two and a half days to read the 870-page behemoth and write the review. A tight deadline, I thought, but not impossible, so I said "yes." It was only then that I realized that the assignment coincided with the annual ALA Conference, which I was committed to attend. Oh, dear. My very full agenda for the conference was already planned, keeping me busy from breakfast until, usually, ten o'clock at night. To make matters worse, the Potter books were embargoed, which meant I couldn't get an advance reading copy. The book's publisher, Scholastic, had promised to deliver a finished copy of the book to my hotel room sometime on Friday. Of course, the book didn't arrive. Which would explain why I was to be found at a neighborhood bookstore at midnight on Friday buying a copy of the book. I got back to my hotel room about 1:00 a.m. and sat up all night reading. Saturday night I did the same, finishing the book at about 6:00 a.m. Sunday morning. My deadline was 9:00 a.m., which gave me roughly three hours to write the review. Reader, I did it. But just barely. My journalism school professors would have been proud.

Once I have the idea, the hardest part of the column is coming up with the opening, the first several lines or paragraph. Sometimes I begin—as I did this essay—with a definition. Thus, I began a column about my house's interior and the books in it with the definition of the word *environment*. Other times I may begin with a quotation. And so I began a column about innovations in young adult literature with a quotation from the biblical book of Ecclesiastes: "And there is no new thing under the sun," for no purpose other than to contradict it: "While I tremble," I accordingly wrote in the opening paragraph, "to disagree with the good book, the fact is there are lots of new things under the sun—if we're talking about the one that shines on the world of young adult literature." But usually I simply plunge right in, trying to hook the reader as quickly as possible. Thus, a column about book collecting began, "Don't tell me you've never dreamed of winning the lottery." From there I went on to write about how I would expand my book collecting hobby if I actually did win the lottery. It was great fun to imagine that, and I hope it was fun for the reader, too. Incidentally, when I wrote the sentence "From there I went on to write . . . ," I almost wrote instead "From there I went on to say . . ." Not exactly a Freudian slip, but certainly one that betrays how I think about the writing style I employ in my columns. I'm told that I write the way I talk, and so I strive for a conversational style and tone. An easy informality is my goal, and that—in my experience—applies to most columnists. This doesn't mean I write in short, declarative sentences.

No, indeed. I often write complex sentences of almost Jamesian length, hoping that punctuation will help clarify the sentence's content and meaning. That explains why colons and semicolons are often my best friends. For example, here's the first sentence of a column about—what else—book collecting: "My book collection has been through a lot during its time with me: relentless relocations, consignment to cold, dark storage units for years on end; threats from leaky roofs and termites; occasional benign neglect or—worse—ham-handed handling by the owner (that would be me); books have been dropped or piled on the floor, exposed to direct sunlight, tossed haphazardly into boxes, stuck in unlikely places (bathtubs or microwave ovens), and yet somehow they have survived." Phew! Logorrhea, thy name is Cart! Aside from excessive wordiness, you might infer several other hallmarks of my style from the above: (1) I never met an adjective I didn't like; (2) I love alliteration; and (3) I dote on parenthetical statements. Hey, they work for me and apparently my editor and readers, too, since I've been doing this for twenty-four years without let or hindrance. Oh, yes, I also like allusions, thus "let or hindrance," which is a legal term that dates back to the eighteenth century. As for the body of the column, one thing I strive for is the seamless segue between paragraphs, with one leading naturally to the next without non sequitur or choppiness. Since I don't work from an outline, I organize material as I go, forced to do so by that consideration of the segue. Which brings us to the last sentence of the column; next to the first, this is the hardest one to write. For the column about winning the lottery, I returned to the topic sentence by concluding with this: "Yes, I know it's all about wish fulfillment, but I can dream, can't I? But first I have to buy a lottery ticket . . ." Oh, yeah, I also like ellipses. As in, if only there were more time and space, I'd write more about columns . . . But this must do for now . . .

And so it must.

INDEX

C

D

E

F

G

H

M

N

O

P

Q

R

S

Z